A BIBLE COMMENTARY FOR LAYMEN

CONFRONTED BY

God's Principles for Daily Living
from 2 Corinthians

DAN BAUMANN

Regal
Books

A Division of GL Publications
Ventura, California, U.S.A.

Rights for publishing this book in other languages are contracted by Gospel Litera-
ture International foundation (GLINT). GLINT also provides technical help for
the adaptation, translation, and publishing of Bible study resources and books in
more than 100 languages worldwide. For further information, contact GLINT,
Post Office Box 6688, Ventura, California 93006, U.S.A., or the publisher.

© Copyright 1985 by Regal Books
A Division of GL Publications
Ventura, California 93006
Printed in U.S.A.

Library of Congress Cataloging in Publication Data applied for.

Baumann, Dan.
    Confronted by love.

    1. Bible. N.T. Corinthians, 2nd—Commentaries.
    2. Christian life—1960-.   I. Title.
BS2675. 3.B34   1985   227'.306   85-2364
ISBN 0-8307-1050-7 (pbk.)

Contents

A coursebook comprising the teacher's manual and reproducible Discovery materials for classes and Bible study groups using this commentary is available from your church supplier.

Being in the Will of God
2 Corinthians 1:1,2

"Paul, an apostle of Christ Jesus by the will of God, and Timothy our brother, to the church of God in Corinth, together with all the saints throughout Achaia: Grace and peace to you from God our Father and the Lord Jesus Christ."

There are two ways to travel. The first is to choose a destination and then plot out a route step by step, all in advance. When my wife and I honeymooned 26 years ago, that was the way we did it. Our destination: Pasadena, California. Before we left Johnson City, Illinois, we had motel reservations, we had provision made, we knew where we would go and where we would stay.

The other way to travel is kind of like a Sunday joy ride. You take off not knowing where you are going; you just follow the wind. Some people travel great distances that way and discover that it is an adventure. However, it can be frustrating when city after city is full of No Vacancy signs. You can go hundreds of miles out of your way before finally finding a place to rest your tired body.

There are two ways to travel; there are two ways to look at the Word of God. This book is going to follow the first. Together, we are going to journey through a book. We will make 13 stops. Our purpose is to discover God's will and truth in Paul's second letter to the Corinthians.

People often study 1 Corinthians and forget about 2 Corinthians, like the ugly sister to whom no one pays attention. Well, we need not overlook 2 Corinthians! It is a great book full of truth about suffering, full of truth about fulfillment, about new life in Christ, about heaven. It is full of encouragement for the discouraged and truth about what makes the Christian life unique. It's all there in 2 Corinthians.

─────── **Understanding 2 Corinthians** ───────

As you begin to study a Bible book there are certain questions to be asked. These questions apply to any study of any book in the Old or New Testaments.

Purpose

What's the purpose? Why was this particular book written? Certain crises had not been settled within the Corinthian church and new ones had arisen. Paul took pen in hand to follow up on his earlier letter. He had sent Titus to Corinth; Titus reported that things were going quite well, but there were a few problems. Chapters 1-7 deal with some of those things that needed to be cleaned up. Chapters 8 and 9 discuss the problem of the poor people in Jerusalem and the Corinthians' promised offering for them. Jerusalem was full of poor, poor people. They were so poor they made students look rich! They were needy people, and Paul reminded the Corinthians of their responsibility to care for these people. In chapters 10-13 Paul anticipated other needs that might arise within the church, and dealt with them.

Date

When was 2 Corinthians written? The date of writing was about A.D. 57, approximately one year after he wrote 1 Corinthians. Paul allowed time for that to settle in and be applied before he followed up. He allowed ample time for the church to be well-established. He wrote 2 Corinthians while on his third missionary journey, from a city where he stayed in public housing—Philippi. That public housing in which Paul stayed is more commonly called jail.

Problems

The critics tell us that there are problems with 2 Corinthians. They tell us that verses 6:14 through 7:1 are interpolated—they have been added to the original. Chapters 8 and 9 are not original, they say; chapters 10 through 13 are not of Paul.

I have some problems with those problems. There is an anti-supernatural presupposition prevalent among some of the critics; they impose upon the text certain standards that I think are irrelevant. They do not give proper place to the supernatural dimension of the Word of God. Textual evidence does not support the theory that Paul did not write 2 Corinthians in its entirety. There is absolutely no textual evidence that proves the letter is not a unit. It is one book, one unit, and the textual evidence historically supports its unity. This book will proceed on the basis that 2 Corinthians has great unity, in spite of what some of its critics may say.

Style

I like the style of 2 Corinthians. It is tough love. It is the kind of book that says, "I love you, but shape up." It reflects the kind of love that loves you enough to confront you, the kind of love that says, "I love you so much that I'm not going to leave you the way you are." It is tough love. In 2 Corinthians, Paul volleys between tenderness and severity, between being tough and being loving.

Paul's love for the Corinthians was that kind of love that I discovered with parents who have older children— 19 and 20 years old—who are on drugs. Counselors and those who have worked with such kids say that parents should not encourage children at that age, who are on drugs, to live at home any longer. Don't provide a place for them to stay. Don't give them clothes. Don't give them food. The most loving thing is to throw them out. If you provide home and food and clothing, you've freed up their money to spend on drugs. They must confront and deal with their problem. They must assume responsibility for it.

I have worked through the process with parents. It was hard on them, but in the end those kids turned around because they were no longer supported in their problem. The parents thought that the loving thing would be to provide for them. In reality, that was unloving. Tough love says, "Face your problems. I'll stand by you, but I won't support your habit." That's the kind of love we discover in 2 Corinthians. Paul says, "I love you, but shape up."

Author

Who wrote 2 Corinthians? There is no question about the author—it is the Apostle Paul. Paul was so wise. The first thing you want to know when you receive a letter is who wrote it. "Paul, an apostle of Christ Jesus by the will of God." Paul wrote at least 13 letters. He always signed them first and then wrote them.

Paul identified himself as an apostle of Christ Jesus by the will of God. His apostleship had been challenged, so

Paul set the record straight. Immediately he established
that not by chance was he an apostle, but he was an apostle by the will of God. False teachers had slipped into the
Corinthian church and had suggested that while they were
apostles, Paul was not. Paul said, "I'm an apostle by the
will of God" to establish his credibility and authenticate the
gospel he had preached to the Corinthians. Throughout 2
Corinthians, Paul wrote not simply as a writer; he wrote
as an apostle in the gospel of Christ which had built the
church at Corinth.

The Recipients

To whom was this letter written? The recipients were
the Corinthians. "To the church of God in Corinth,
together with all the saints throughout Achaia." Corinth
was a large, vulgar city—a city so vulgar that Las Vegas
would look like a sleepy little rural community in compari-
son. The people of Corinth had mastered the art of sensu-
ality and sinfulness; they almost had it patented. In the
midst of this vulgarity was this little island of believers.
Unfortunately, too much of Corinth was in the church.

Second Corinthians was written also to the larger area,
Achaia, which suggests that this was a circular letter, pri-
marily to the Corinthians but also to believers in that
whole area. A traveler today may have difficulty finding
Achaia. Greece may be a little easier to find, and that basically is the area in question. Achaia was modern Greece
plus a little more, but it at least included Greece.

The Salutation

Paul's salutation was not merely, "How are you?" It
was, "Grace and peace to you from God our Father and
the Lord Jesus Christ." Paul describes God's grace as His
redeeming favor conferred by God on men. The result of
this grace is peace, welfare, health in God, reconciliation

with God. Together, "grace and peace" denote all that we have because of God's initiative in our lives. Grace makes us a reconciled people experiencing the peace of God.

—————————— **Understanding God's Will** ——————————

Paul described himself as an apostle of Christ Jesus by the will of God. What is God's will? How do you understand God's will? How do you deal with it? It is one of those subjects that often becomes a question of great mystery for Christians; we want to know how to discover it. Once it is discovered, how do we make peace with it? Paul was certain that all he did was in the will and purpose of God. He did what he did because it was God's plan. He was an apostle because that was His program.

Not Necessarily Easy to Experience

The first thing that we must note immediately is that God's will is not necessarily easy to experience. No one would have chosen to experience what Paul experienced. Think about what he went through. He experienced hardship, he suffered a stoning, he was abused, he was insulted, he went through multiple imprisonments. Paul experienced all of that and yet had the audacity to say, "All things work together for good to those who love God, to those who are the called according to His purpose" (Rom. 8:28, *NKJV*). In a recent memorial service at my church it was mentioned that the will of God has areas of hurt, pain, and mystery that cannot quite be understood. One wonders how that all fits. Paul said all things work together. It's kind of like biscuits. Biscuits—oh, warm biscuits. Mmmm, that does sound good. But think about the individual ingredients. Would you eat them individually? Of course not! The ingredients have little value until they are mixed together. Yet, it is not enough to just mix them together. They must go through the heat. When all the ingredients of life have gone through the heat of life, we can look back and say, "All things work together for good to them who are called according to His purpose." All the individual ingredients may not look good for you, you would not have chosen them, but if it is God's will, it is right although not necessarily easy.

Not Necessarily Full-time Service

God's will is not necessarily full-time service. You may be tempted to look with great envy upon the folks who serve on your pastoral staff and say, "Oh to be in God's work, to enjoy that. Then I would be a fulfilled person." God's will for some is to do that; God's will for most is not. There is nothing more miserable than being a pastor when you should have been a teacher or an engineer or a salesman. God's will is individually understood, and you are gifted accordingly, you are led accordingly. There are people who are as much in the will of God today as carpenters, as Billy Graham is at the height of a crusade. God's will is for you a distinctive experience. God ordains carpenters, electricians, salesmen, professional people, and engineers, and God ordains you to your ministry.

I have felt for some time that the choice of Matthias was not right. It is recorded for us in the book of Acts. The apostles had lost one of their number; they were down to eleven. You know the sad story of Judas. Now they had to replace him. They prayed and drew straws. The life of Matthias does not look like the sterling life we see in the other apostles. I have felt that the choosing of Matthias was like a bunch of Christians today praying and then throwing dice, or praying and taking a name out of a hat.

God's will is not necessarily being in full-time Christian service. Maybe Matthias should have been a fisherman.

God's will for you is not necessarily full-time Christian service.

God's Will—Basically Clear

Is God's will basically clear? For Paul it unfolded, and he understood it. He walked in it and lived by it. There are three areas of God's will for us that are basically clear.

Salvation. Second Peter 3:9 says that God does not want anyone to perish but that all would come to repentance. God's purpose for you is that you would know His life, His salvation—that you would be born anew by the Spirit of God. If you've never done that, that's one part of His will that is abundantly clear. He wants you to be His child by an act of personal faith. That is His will.

It is often said that the best things in life are free. I buy that. It's the second-best things in life that cost you money. Houses, clothes, cars, those sort of things. Those are second-best.

What's best in life? Friends, love, salvation. You can't improve on them; those are the best. And they're free. You would have everything you need if you would claim it. Salvation is the best of them all. God says, "I love you and I give this to you. By grace you are saved through faith, not of yourself—it is the gift of God. Purchased at great price, but offered freely" (see Eph. 2:8). The best things in life *are* free. Salvation in Jesus Christ. That's the best.

Obedience. That is always His will. Matthew 22 talks about loving the Lord your God with your whole being—body, soul, spirit—your whole self, wholeheartedly, and loving your neighbor as yourself. That is obedience. One Sunday night after I had preached about the conditions of answered prayer, someone met me at the door and said, "It all kind of boils down to obedience, doesn't it?" Right! You can't get far beyond that. If you want to know God's will, if you want to walk in it, it takes obedience to do it.

Talents. God's spiritual gifts, those gifts of grace, are listed in three books. Romans chapter 12, 1 Corinthians 12, and Ephesians 4. From the Romans 12:6-8 listing you need to note this: "We have different gifts, according to the grace given us." God gives them to us by grace; they are grace gifts—*charismata*. "If a man's gift is prophesying, let him use it in proportion to his faith. If it is serving, let him serve; if it is teaching, let him teach; if it is encouraging, let him encourage; if it is contributing to the needs of others, let him give generously; if it is leadership, let him govern diligently; if it is showing mercy, let him do it cheerfully." You have it—use it!

God's will is that the gift or gifts you have be used. It is never God's will to treat your gifts like an autographed major league baseball—to put them up on the mantle and say, "Those are my gifts." Get out and use them. Gifts are distributed sovereignly by God to be used, not to be admired. They are to be used for the benefit of all of us. If in fact the church has its weakness, if in fact the church has its deficiency, it is not because God has not gifted us. It is because we have not used the gifts we have. It is always God's purpose that you take what He has given you and use it for the common good. Always! Are you doing that? That is basically clear.

Salvation—that is His will. Obedience—that is His will. The talents you have are to be used—that's His will. No mystery there. It's a long way toward understanding His will.

How do you know God's will? By reading it. The Word of God has been given. His will is not simply reserved in heaven as an abstract statement removed and distant from us; it has been given in a book called the Bible. You can read His will; it is there. You discover His will by doing it. You may say, "That's strange reasoning. Don't you discover it and do it?" No, you do it and discover it.

One day I was at Forest Home Christian Conference Center. I was to return to the Los Angeles area but it was foggy. I started on that meandering two-lane road. There was a white line down the center; I stayed to the right of that. Now I could have waited up at the top until the fog cleared, but that may have been morning. So I began the journey, and I watched that line. The fog was heavy so I drove slowly. When the fog would lift, I would speed it up. When it set in, I would slow down, but I kept inching and moving along. As I moved along I discovered more as the road unfolded and opened up in front of me. God's will is like that. You take what you know of His will and you walk in it. Then He unfolds and opens up and lifts and clears and helps us understand. You discover it by doing it. You don't sit around waiting to understand His will. You take what you know of His will and walk in it and then He unfolds more for you. That's really the translation of Romans 12. You discover in practice what the will of God is. Good and acceptable and perfect. Paul said, "I'm an apostle by the will of God." Do you live by that same will? Good and acceptable and perfect. For in the living of it you discover fulfillment; you discover great joy; you discover that all things are working together for good, because you are living according to His purpose. Do you know it? Now do it.

Questions for Discussion

1. What does "tough love" mean to you? What kinds of situations call for loving confrontation?

2. Which areas of God's will are clear to you? Which are not?

3. Which areas of God's will are easiest to accept? Which are hardest?

4. Have you followed God's will for your salvation, obedience, and use of your talents? What has hindered you? What must you do to follow Him?

2

When You Feel Inadequate
2 Corinthians 2:14–3:11

"But thanks be to God, who always leads us in triumphal procession in Christ and through us spreads everywhere the fragrance of the knowledge of him. For we are to God the aroma of Christ among those who are being saved and those who are perishing. To the one we are the smell of death; to the other, the fragrance of life. And who is equal to such a task? Unlike so many, we do not peddle the word of God for profit. On the contrary, in Christ we speak before God with sincerity, like men sent from God.

"Are we beginning to commend ourselves again? Or do we need, like some people, letters of recommendation to you or from you? You yourselves are our letter, written on our hearts, known and read by everybody. You show that you are a letter from Christ, the result of our ministry, written not with ink but with the Spirit of the living God, not on tablets of stone but on tablets of human hearts.

"Such confidence as this is ours through Christ before God. Not that we are competent to claim anything for ourselves, but our competence comes from God. He has made us competent as ministers of a new covenant—not of the letter but of the Spirit; for the letter kills, but the Spirit gives life."

A few years ago three couples took a trip traveling from a large island to a very small island. As they checked in they gave their tickets to a man who took them and also wrote down each person's weight. He then told them to go into a waiting room. When he came back, he asked them to follow him. They walked across the airstrip and past a number of large, magnificent planes, finally coming to a rather ancient, single-engine plane. As they were boarding he seated them according to their individual weights so that the plane was balanced. Then he told them about the safety provisions of that plane and what to do in an emergency. Afterwards he closed the door, put the luggage on the plane, stepped into the cockpit, and flew to the little island. When they landed, he opened the door, got them out of the plane, unloaded their luggage, and then went in to the reception desk to check in the returning passengers. He did it all! He was flight attendant, baggage carrier, pilot, and clerk.

I think of that story when I read this text. The job description of the Christian calls for doing it all. Did you notice that? Chapter 2:14-17 tell us that we are the ones who declare the gospel. That's a big job. That's a big assignment. In chapter 3, verses 1-3, he says we are to *be* the gospel. We are to talk it and we are to walk it. We are to share it and we are to incarnate the gospel. Is it little wonder then that Paul asks in verse 16, "Who is equal to such a task?" This is a huge assignment and makes us feel inadequate.

─────── **An Overwhelming Challenge** ───────

Paul begins in verse 14 by suggesting something that has really blessed his heart. He is just bursting as he says, "Thanks be to God, who always leads us in triumphal procession in Christ." What is he talking about? Paul had just gotten word from Titus that things were going well at Corinth. Here was a church that had discovered all sins available and tried them. The world was not to be in the church, but that is exactly where the world was. When they ran out of existing sins, they had invented new ones. Altogether it was a depressing scene at Corinth. So Paul had taken pen in hand and in 1 Corinthians had addressed these problems, interlacing them with encouragement and urging the people to get on with the task. Get together; don't be divided! There has been immorality; straighten it out. Your marriages have been bad; get them back together. Your worship has been disruptive; make certain that you do that right. Let's get with it!

Titus comes along saying it's working! It's happening! Paul is just about ready to burst the buttons on his tunic! He is thanking God and rejoicing in what the gospel is doing at Corinth. He then expands to include the magnificent statement about the gospel in its application and expression in the whole world. He uses Corinth as illustration but application is for the whole church. "Thanks be to God, who always leads us in triumphal procession in Christ and through us spreads everywhere the fragrance of the knowledge of him."

To Share the Faith

Picture the scene—a street in Rome. Down the street

comes the general, wearing all the braids and decorations. He is triumphantly marching at the front with his soldiers following behind. This is pomp-and-circumstance day. They have just won the battle and they are marching victoriously through town. Behind them come the defeated, in chains, walking dejectedly. They have been conquered. Then come the high priests, waving their censers, and the beautiful aroma of burning incense and spices wafts its way across the city streets. Paul says that the gospel is like that. The knowledge of Christ is an aroma that spreads itself through the city. When you share the gospel it comes as a marvelous fragrance from God. The next verse says we are the aroma of Christ to God. We not only share the fragrance, but we become that beautiful fragrance before God Himself.

When we share the gospel it immediately causes division. Verses 15 and 16 say we share it "among those who are being saved and those who are perishing. To the one we are the smell of death; to the other, the fragrance of life." You see, it's bad news for some, good news for others. Paul is saying to some, rather than being a beautiful aroma, it stinks; it is the smell of death. The gospel alienates. But for those who accept it, it comes as marvelous fragrance.

David Jeremiah has written a book in which he talks about a sculptor who worked with two pieces.[1] One was clay, the other was wax. In his rush he inadvertently left them exposed to the sun over the weekend. When he came back on Monday he discovered that the wax had melted and a stain was all that was left, but the clay had become hard as a rock. David Jeremiah says the gospel does that. With some, it comes to soften; with some, to harden. The same gospel, based on the way it is received, does radically different things; it divides people. Our assignment is to share it, and others will respond as they choose. It is good news to those who believe; it is bad news to those who reject.

I want you to notice something in verse 15: it is happening "among those who are being saved, and those who are perishing." *Being saved* and *perishing* are both present participles. One is passive, one is active. *Who are being saved* is a passive present participle. Salvation is an act of God being done to us. We are passive and respond by faith. God makes us new; we don't make ourselves new. But *who are perishing* is an active present participle. They are perishing based on their actions. They have chosen to perish and not believe. Now, that is very important.

I was invited to San Diego State to share with Students for Jesus. One of the students came up to me afterwards asking, "Is it fair for God, who knows all things, who designs all things, and who determines all things, to bring people into the world that He knows are condemned to hell? Is that fair? How do you respond to that?" First, God is sovereign, God does choose, God is in control, God is in charge. He is Lord over His creation, and He is Lord over people. On the other hand, there is written across the Old and New Testaments a statement about the freedom of humanity. All of us stand responsible and accountable. And however you deal with sovereignty, you must accept the fact that there is also freedom God has granted so we choose either to believe or we choose not to believe. And this text is saying they have chosen to perish by their own actions. It was not that they were destined for hell, but they have chosen to perish.

I take sovereignty and human freedom to be a paradox. A paradox that is eternal is in error. A paradox that is temporal is simply one that we can't reconcile because we aren't bright enough. It will be reconciled and is obviously in the heart and the mind of God. People have choice and they choose their destiny. I am convinced the text is saying that. Now Paul moves on to say we not only have to share that message but we have to model the faith.

To Model the Faith

In chapter 3 Paul is talking about letters of reference. In the first century, as in our day, a letter of reference would open up a job for you or open up a situation for you. When you went off to college or went off to a job, you may have had letters of reference. Paul is referring to the heretics that had come into the Corinthian church. When the papyrus was opened, speaking of the people in glowing terms, the church took them in. They were welcomed on the basis of letters of reference even though the references were invalid. And Paul says, do I need letters of reference? No. Wherever I go in Corinth, you are my letters. Your life is an indication that the gospel does what I claim it's to do. You are my Epistles; you are little living Bibles running all over Corinth.

Paul is reminding us that the gospel takes on flesh. Those who believe are changed. You and I go into our world and we face people who have no Bible. They may have one but they don't read it. But if they see us, they can read a chapter a day. Is that heavy? Are you ready for that? If you knew the people at work would not have any other Bible experience except for your life, are they likely to come to faith? You are their Epistle, their living Bible. Are you tempted to say, "I can't handle that." I think all of us would have to acknowledge there are times in our spiritual lives that may not lead people to Christ. There are times in the way that we relate to our family that may not set a good example.

———————— A Workable Solution ————————

When you put real live people in a real live world and

tell real live people who are not Christians that you are the
Bible, that's a big assignment. We are tempted to say, with
Paul, "Who is equal to such a task?" Fortunately, Paul
doesn't leave us discouraged without the outcome and he
moves very quickly into a workable solution.

Accept Our Inadequacy

First, we are to accept our inadequacy. Notice verse 5,
"Not that we are competent to claim anything for ourselves, but our competence comes from God." Paul
begins by acknowledging the fact that we aren't capable,
we aren't competent, we cannot do what we were called to
do. We need the Lord. It is only when we begin to look at
our lives and the responsibility and the privilege we have,
and say, "I can't," that we have the possibility of doing it.
We begin with incompetence.

Acknowledge His Adequacy

Next, look to His adequacy. Paul moves on to say, "but
our competence comes from God. He has made us competent as ministers of a new covenant." All the inadequacy
you discover in yourself and I discover in myself simply
becomes the foundation upon which He places His
resources and His competence to do what we cannot do.
But if we walk through life acting competently, we only
prove our incompetence. Those who acknowledge their
incompetence become candidates for competence. God
only uses those who acknowledge their need. This concept may be difficult to comprehend. Let me suggest three
things to help put it together.

Be sure of your faith. Competence is a relationship. You
don't go from incompetence to competence without walking through the door of salvation. Jesus Christ offers you
competence as part of the provision of eternal salvation.
When you link your life with the eternal God through faith,

you then become a branch and vine combination and His life flows through you. Competence comes as He is in us. "I am in Christ," says Paul. "I am crucified with Christ, nevertheless I live yet not I but Christ lives in me. The life which I now live in the flesh I live by the faithfulness of the Son of God who loved me and gave himself for me" (see Gal. 2:20). That's relationship! If you've never made that relationship a reality, do it now by simply acknowledging your need and trusting Him as personal Saviour. In faith let Him come into your life. That's where competence begins. It is related to the source of our life.

Rest in His grace. If He is adequate, don't be frantic. Don't run around as if it all depends on your ability alone. You are in Him. One of the marks of those who trust is rest. When I see Christians running around as if it all depends on them, they have not learned to rest. And when you rest in Him you learn to rejoice in Him. I have been reading the biographies of the men that I have admired for a long time. Men like Martin Luther and Charles Haddon Spurgeon, who were two great preachers and theologians who moved countries for God. Both were men who had a marvelous sense of joy in their lives. Both of them found that whenever they preached, they had to watch themselves and guard against telling too many funny things, because they were overflowing with joy. When the Lord comes and you are resting in Him, there is a joy which you must have to hold in at times because that's what He provides if you truly have found Him to be your competence. You rest in Him, which is really a statement of faith, and you rejoice in that relationship.

Make yourself available to God. Begin your day praying, "Lord, I don't know what is ahead of me today, but I am yours, and I want to be available." You don't have to lay out a game plan, scheduling time to talk to this person, or deciding, I'm going to do this for God today. Simply make yourself available to God. Let the Lord bring into your life those people who need you. Let those natural relationships in your everyday activities be the place where you just share Him and live out your life in Him. Relax, He has come to touch you and use you and enable you. Plastic saints or predictable statements in our world are not very influential. The ones most influential for God are those down-to-earth, natural people who have allowed God to change them and to use them. Be relaxed in the world, for Jesus' sake; just share and just be. The Lord will enable us to be what we could never be on our own.

I look at His assignment for us. That's a tough job description. Not only am I called to share the gospel—that beautiful fragrance of life—but I am called to be an Epistle known and read by everybody; and I say, Who's equal to that? Paul comes along and says, "Dan Baumann, you are not competent, but the Lord says, 'I want to make you competent. I want to live my life through you, commit yourself to me, rest in me, make yourself available; I'll use you, trust me.'" Could you do that?

Questions for Discussion

1. What aroma does your spiritual life produce? Does it attract or repel others?

2. Are there people whose lives are "letters of recommendation" for your Christianity? Who are they?

3. How accurately does your life reflect the truth of the gospel? How can you improve in this area?

4. Have you made yourself available to God today? Will you?

NOTE
1. David Jeremiah, *Growing Strong in the Seasons of Life* (Portland, Oregon: Multnomah Press, 1983).

3

A Fantastic Message
2 Corinthians 3:12—4:6

"Therefore, since we have such a hope, we
are very bold. We are not like Moses, who
would put a veil over his face to keep the Israel-
ites from gazing at it while the radiance was fad-
ing away. But their minds were made dull, for to
this day the same veil remains when the old
covenant is read. It has not been removed,
because only in Christ is it taken away. Even to
this day when Moses is read, a veil covers their
hearts. But whenever anyone turns to the
Lord, the veil is taken away. Now the Lord is
the Spirit, and where the Spirit of the Lord is,
there is freedom. And we, who with unveiled
faces all reflect the Lord's glory, are being
transformed into his likeness with ever-
increasing glory, which comes from the Lord,
who is the Spirit."

Do you remember the greatest decision you have ever made? What is the most exciting announcement that you have ever heard? How did you feel when you heard the news? Has it been etched upon your memory so you will never, never forget it? Remember the television series "The Millionaire"? A person with very simple means is unexpectedly told, "You are now a millionaire." The camera would zoom in on the face, as it registered great delight and excitement, as if this were the greatest moment in this person's life. A sudden transformation from a nobody to a millionaire. This was great news!

As Paul discusses great news, he says, the great news is the good news. The best news of all is the fact that God in Christ takes people who are alienated and reconciles them. He takes people who are at a distance and brings them near. He takes folks who are away from God and brings them near. He takes folks who are away from God and brings them into the family of God. He takes people who are burdened with sin and forgives them. "God was in Christ, reconciling the world unto himself." Paul says, this is good news—the good news that we declare. We don't preach ourselves, he says, but we preach Jesus Christ as Lord. As Paul goes on he says that great, fantastic message is both eye-opening and life-transforming. Notice how he begins.

The Gospel Is Eye-Opening

Paul talks about Moses, saying there are two classifications of people in all the world: those who are blind and those who see. There are no other choices. Moses, when he went up onto the mountain, received the glory of God that was reflected even in his face. As he came down, he put a veil over his face so as the glory faded away it would not be an observable fact. He was covered. Have you ever noticed the change in a person who works in an office and has a middle-America, white, pale look, who gets two weeks of vacation and spends them on the beach and comes back with a golden brown tan; then in the succeeding days slowly becomes white and anemic again and the glory fades. I am not exactly sure what Moses' glory looked like, but it was a radiance that had been an expression of meeting God face-to-face. Moses wore the veil so that you wouldn't see the paleness of his face returning once again. The glory was hidden as it faded.

But then Paul goes on to say that that same kind of veil is over the eyes of the unbeliever; notice verse 14: "their minds were made dull, for to this day the same veil remains when the old covenant is read. It has not been removed, because only in Christ is it taken away." The old covenant was the law. The new covenant is in Jesus Christ where He becomes once and for all the total, finished work of God. He is saying that anybody who has not come to experience Christ is living with that veil, living under the old covenant. Not that it was wrong, but that it was incomplete. Only in Jesus Christ is it completed richly, fully, and totally. If the old revelation in Moses was a stepping-stone to glory, the revelation in Jesus Christ is the very summit of glory. But those who have not met Christ still have that veil over their faces. How come? How can bright, alert, thoughtful, even religious people, be blinded? Have you not talked with people wishing you could pull them into the Kingdom, and they just can't see? Why can't they believe it? In every other area of their life, they seem to do so well—everything is under control, everything is organized, they have keen minds and sensitive hearts, but they are blind. There is a clue in the text: the veil is blinding. Verse 14 tells us their minds are dull and so is their understanding. They just can't see. Paul explains in verse 15 and says a veil covers their hearts when the old covenant is read. There is spiritual blindness in both the mind and the heart which prevents them from seeing.

Furthermore, Paul tells us to whom that blindness comes. Look at verse 4 of chapter 4, where he tells us: "The god of this age has blinded the minds of unbelievers," which includes everybody from reprobate to religious, from convict to Nicodemus. Unbelief leads to blindness. In Christ there is sight. Satan has been at work, and the work of Satan is to keep you from seeing the truth, to blind you, to keep you in unbelief. In John he's called "the prince of this world"; in Ephesians he's called "the prince of the power of the air"; here he's called "the god of this age." Robert Lewis Stevenson said, "One cold windy day, I met Satan in the Caledonian Railway Station in Edinburgh." You meet him everywhere. He's active, blinding people to spiritual truth. Good people, and yet Satan is at work in their lives. I am convinced that it is not only Satan who blinds but sometimes we blind ourselves. How does that happen? There are several ways.

Disobedience. We choose our own veil. We know the truth and we choose not to do it. That's the veil of disobedience.

Acculturated. We get caught up with those around us and become acculturated, reflecting a whole people that have no place for God. That happens all the time. There is the story of the young Indian boy who had prairie chicken eggs. One day he found an eagle egg. He kept all of these eggs and brought warmth to them so that in time they broke open and there were little chickens and an eagle. The chickens started to grow and the eagle started to grow, and they lived together. They thought they were all one kind. One day these little prairie chickens, who could fly about 10 feet and then flutter to the ground, were with the eagle when some eagles soared overhead. The little chickens were out there going, "Wow, can they fly," and the eagle said, "Isn't that incredible." Sadly the eagle died, never getting 10 feet off the ground. He thought he was a prairie chicken. A lot of people just let the world around them squeeze them into its mold, going with the flow, and never turning upwards, never turning to God. I met a lovely woman yesterday and I asked her, "Where do you go to church?" And she said, "I'm embarrassed, I don't, it's been years." She was a good, moral, lovely lady and yet she was caught up with the flow.

Foolishness. We are sometimes just plain foolish. We do foolish things instead of doing the right things to understand what God would have for us. Did you read the story of the 70-foot commercial fishing boat, whose driver plowed into the pier at Shelter Island? He was given a ticket for drunken driving. Do you know what pier he chose—the Harbor Patrol Dock. My guess is he would never pick that pier, but he made a foolish decision while he was intoxicated, and did something that was just plain dumb. There are a lot of people who make foolish decisions and never choose to discover the truth or to see what Christ has for them.

Unteachable Spirit. There are those with an unteachable spirit. I remember one man who used to sit in the audience on Sunday mornings challenging me to teach him something. I figured if the Spirit of God didn't do it, I would never get through because he was convinced that I wouldn't. That unteachable spirit is very common in our world. Don't tell me. That's a choice of a spiritual veil to keep you from the truth.

Here's the good news: "But whenever anyone turns to the Lord, the veil is taken away" (3:16). Paul is saying if a person would turn to Jesus Christ spiritual blindness would be gone and the veil would be lifted. He has a little of his testimony behind that statement. When Paul is talking, he is reflecting upon his own past. He was a good man, a righteous man, a godly man by the religious standards of his day. A Pharisee doing the right thing, but just as blind as he could be. Then one day he met Jesus, and he saw, and it was all new, and he was changed. For you see, just as Moses lifted the veil when he went in to see the Lord, so it is with us. When we meet the Lord, our veil is lifted and we see Him—all of a sudden. Once I was blind, now I see—the gospel is eye-opening!

──────── **The Gospel Is Life-Changing** ────────

"Now the Lord is the Spirit, and where the Spirit of the Lord is, there is freedom" (v. 17). There are two things that happen that are life-changing.

Freedom

First of all we experience freedom. Freedom, what is that all about? I wish I could introduce you to Mary Stauffer or Eunice Crownhold. They are two ladies who were kidnapped. Mary Stauffer, a missionary, was kidnapped in St. Paul, Minnesota, along with her daughter Beth, and kept for weeks by her captors. Most of the time they were chained in a closet. Mary could tell you what freedom is like. For one day she escaped, unshackled. Eunice Crownhold could tell you being captive in a trunk of a car for long, long hours is an incredible experience, and when you are released, you know what freedom is like. Yet their experiences were not as bad as being chained and bound in sin. For you see, people are then chained to their guilt, chained to their destiny, and chained to the dominion of sin. There is the freedom that they don't have, that we have, to be free from guilt, free from our past, free from the law, and free from anything that would shackle us. We have been released and the chains have fallen off.

Then we have freedom of access to God. In the old

covenant Moses represented the people and only the high priest could go into the holy of holies. Now there is freedom from those limitations. We have immediate access and at any time we can talk to God. In the middle of a frustrated working day, wondering what to do next, we can just talk to Him and go right into the holy of holies. We have that freedom. In the middle of those troublesome hours as we toss and turn at night, wondering what in the world will we do, we can just open up our lives to Him and be in the holy of holies immediately. Freedom of access, that's ours. Freedom to worship, freedom from fear of death, and freedom from the shackles of guilt. The glorious freedom of the people of God. That's ours!

Transformation

Notice the ways Paul writes in verse 18, "We, who with unveiled faces all reflect the Lord's glory, are being transformed . . . . " The word "transformed" is the same word used of Jesus Christ describing His transfiguration. Remember, Peter, James, and John were with Jesus on the mountain. As He is transfigured, Peter gets so excited he wants to build three little booths up there, three little tabernacles, three little places to memorialize it. His heart was bubbling over for he had met the transfigured Lord and been part of that marvelous experience. It had been such a thrilling thing to him that he had to do something about it. Well, that word describes your life. In the gospel, you are transfigured, you are transformed, you are radically changed.

In the *New International Version,* the word "beholding" or seeing was omitted. I wish it had been included. "But we all, with unveiled face beholding as in a mirror the glory of the Lord, are being transformed . . . " (3:18, *NASB*). There is a connection of cause and effect, those beholding are transformed. Seeing changes us. Here's the principle. We reflect what we respect, or whom we respect! What you choose as a model will begin to define your life. Whom you choose for an image bearer, or a person that you emulate, as you continue to behold, your life will begin to echo that life.

Remember years ago when the Beatles became popular? Did you notice how the young people's hair style changed to a Beatle haircut? Then along came punk rock—and the punk rock musicians, with their hair color and hair style? It is not exactly a middle-class American hair style. Well, teens reflect what they respect. We did it in seminary years ago. There was a time when all the seminarians were going out and buying red Bibles because Billy Graham preached out of a red Bible. We reflect what we respect. Now that is not always bad; it can be very good. It can be very challenging too. If your children respect you, they will reflect you. As we continue to gaze, to focus, to worship, and to build our lives around Him, we will be like the Lord we worship. Beholding, we are transformed. The contemplation and the worship of our Lord makes us increasingly Christlike.

Who is this for? Not for a privileged group. This is for anybody. Paul says open the door so that all may come. No longer is it a lawgiver or a high priest that alone enjoys the benefits. It is for all! People who allow their lives to be touched by Jesus Christ can enjoy the transformation and experience the great freedom of the people of God. It's for anyone, not only for the privileged class. But we have to respond to it and receive it. Julius Caesar, on his way to Rome, was approached by a messenger who had an important letter. The messenger urged him, "Please read it immediately! It contains an important message." Caesar tucked it in his belt unread, and went off to Rome in his chariot where he was assassinated. That letter had warned him of that assassination. When they found his dead body, the unopened letter was still tucked in his tunic.

The message of the gospel is news we need to do something about. We can go through life and not open the message, keeping the veil. But the moment we turn to Jesus Christ that veil is lifted and we see. Our lives are made new. Let it happen.

Questions for Discussion

1. How was learning about the gospel an eye-opening experience for you?

2. Is your spirit teachable? What barriers have you erected to protect yourself from the truth? Will you allow God to destroy those barriers through His Word?

3. How has the gospel changed your life? Are those changes visible in your daily life?

4. What or whom have you chosen to model your life after? Are you reflecting what you respect?

Treasure in Fragile Containers
2 Corinthians 4:7-19

"But we have this treasure in jars of clay to show that this all-surpassing power is from God and not from us. We are hard pressed on every side, but not crushed; perplexed, but not in despair; persecuted, but not abandoned; struck down, but not destroyed. We always carry around in our body the death of Jesus, so that the life of Jesus may also be revealed in our body. For we who are alive are always being given over to death for Jesus' sake, so that his life may be revealed in our mortal body. So then, death is at work in us, but life is at work in you.

"It is written: 'I believed; therefore I have spoken.' With that same spirit of faith we also believe and therefore speak, because we know that the one who raised the Lord Jesus from the dead will also raise us with Jesus and present us with you in his presence. All this is for your benefit, so that the grace that is reaching more and more people may cause thanksgiving to overflow to the glory of God.

"Therefore we do not lose heart. Though outwardly we are wasting away, yet inwardly we are being renewed day by day. For our light and momentary troubles are achieving for us an eternal glory that far outweighs them all. So we fix our eyes not on what is seen, but on what is unseen. For what is seen is temporary, but what is unseen is eternal."

I recently saw an eight-page multicolored advertising piece entitled, "Be Beautiful." One of the items that caught my attention promoted perfumes. Let me describe three of them. The first is described as "a mysterious, oriental fragrance with a touch of Paris," at $160 an ounce; the second fragrance is "a classic with bright floral notes enriched by warm amber and spice." It sold for $165 an ounce. The next, "an orchestration of 175 natural ingredients, including the rarest oils from jasmine and orange blossoms," a mere $275 an ounce. I was stunned by the prices. But what struck me the most was this marvelous expensive fragrance came in little glass vials perhaps costing no more than 50 cents each. If those vials were dropped on a hard surface, they would shatter; and if they were exposed to extreme cold, they would crack. There they were, fragile, rather inexpensive vials containing great, expensive treasure. That is what the text talks about. It says that in fragile, frail people, who are like earthenware jars, or glass vials, are contained the riches of God's grace in the gospel.

We may ask why such a glorious message is in such an inglorious container? Notice verse 7, "to show that this all-surpassing power is from God and not from us." To avoid getting the impression that the glory of the gospel has to do with the glory of the one who experienced it, Paul reminds us that we have fragile containers in which is contained all the riches of what God is doing in the gospel. The praise is His, and the frailty is ours. We experience His grace, not because of us, but because of what He has put in us. The treasure in fragile containers.

Now, as Paul develops this, there is an interesting volley between the trials our fragile bodies contain and experience, and the triumphs we experience because of the gospel. Have you been to a tennis match where rather than watching the ball you watch the audience following the movement of the ball from left to right? This is the text: trial—triumph—trial—triumph—trial—triumph, and the volley between these two phenomena in life. It is a fact that you are going to experience some tough days, but you are also going to have the triumph. Let's look at the trials first.

───────────── **The Trials of Life** ─────────────

Paradox

"We are hard pressed on every side, but not crushed; perplexed, but not in despair; persecuted, but not abandoned; struck down, but not destroyed" (v. 8). Students understand what Paul is talking about when they're in the middle of exam week at the end of the semester. That feeling that your world is just coming down, and you grit your teeth and hold on! Paul says there are four trials. Someone has suggested that these are the ongoing stages of a soldier in conflict.

Pressured, but not hemmed in. The word "pressured" is the word used for crushing grapes. See the grapes giving up their juices as they are crushed. This is how you feel when you are caught in that kind of a vise. The world crushes down upon you and you feel pressure. It is the pressure you feel from economics, from real estate, from all the interactions in working with colleagues, all the things you have in terms of maintaining your own family and your own responsibilities. You say, "Wow, I feel the pressure."

The text also reminds us that we are pressured but not hemmed in. There is a way out. "No temptation has seized you except what is common to man. And God is faithful; he will not let you be tempted beyond what you can bear. But when you are tempted, he will also provide a way out so that you can stand up under it" (1 Cor. 10:13). That's the ongoing faithful message of the Word of God. You may feel pressures but there is always some way out. Pressured, but not hemmed in.

Do you know the story of Linda Downs? Linda Downs finished the New York marathon, and by the time she did most of the folks had gone home—hours before. A few were there, including the television cameras from "That's Incredible." The President himself called Linda Downs. Why? She had crossed the line for the 26-mile marathon on crutches! Linda Downs is an encouragement to all of us who feel at times that we can't run it, that we can't do it because the pressure is too great. And the Word tells us that is not so. We are pressured, but there is a way out.

Perplexed, but not without hope. The word "perplexed" comes from two words, "narrow" and "space." Get the picture of being in a small room and feeling boxed in like being in a phone booth, feeling at wit's end. This is the picture here. You are perplexed and you just don't know if you are going to get out. You are at your wit's end. But not at hope's end.

Some years ago I went down to San Quentin in Baja California, about 200 miles south of San Diego. I went down there for the first time with four or five others in a little private plane from Los Angeles. We landed and spent a day with missionaries and had an excellent time. They challenged us and showed us their little village ministries, especially the new chapel they were constructing. Late in the afternoon we boarded the plane and took off. As we got up into the air and began to move towards the Los Angeles area we were surrounded by heavy black clouds. Our plane was not equipped with all the instrumentation needed and so we were flying by sight. We would go through these solid clouds. There was a 10-minute period without a break. And we felt that at any moment, a plane could pop out of the next cloud and we'd collide.

Finally, it cleared. That's the picture in the text.

You feel hemmed in, and it is dark and there is no way out and then the cloud lifts. You do not need to feel there is no hope. You may be at your wit's end, but there is hope, always. God has so worked our lives.

Persecuted, but not abandoned. Sometimes you feel the pressure taking the form of persecution. Because of your faith you may encounter difficult times. One of my parishioners was dismissed from her job because she was vocal in her faith; because she told people about the Lord on her job. That is a form of persecution. It may be the silent treatment, or it may take other forms, but you feel a loner because of your faith. Scripture says we are persecuted but not abandoned. You may cry, "Oh, Lord, I am alone, I am all alone." Then He reminds you, this is not true. Other believers may be available but certainly the Lord is always there. Joan of Ark had friends who left her when they should have stayed. Out of that experience of being all alone, Joan of Ark wrote: "It is better to be alone with God, His friendship will not fail me, nor His love fail me. In His strength, I will dare and I will dare and I will dare until I die." Joan of Ark was saying, "Persecuted, perhaps, but not abandoned—not alone."

Struck down (pummeled) but not destroyed. You will

notice that the first three are *p*'s—pressured, perplexed, and persecuted. No pastor would ever allow the fourth one to start with an *s,* so struck down means pummeled. Pummeled, but not knocked out. You are beaten upon, but not for the 10 count. You see that right coming and you take it, and then when you are ready for the right, you get hit by the left. Even when you think you have been beaten, you get up. God's grace is available. God says, "I don't want you knocked out." He is going to provide for you, and up you will come.

Many of us have the impression that Paul is speaking out of the Lystra experience, where Paul was stoned. (We have to re-interpret that in our day and say he was rocked, because stoned means something else.) But they took rocks and did him in, and left him for dead. When they all left, Paul got up and left town. He did not want to hang around there any more. The picture is of someone who has been knocked down but not knocked out—someone who rises again. God says that you are going to face trials and you are going to face tests. Don't be surprised by them. You will be perplexed, but not in despair; persecuted, but not abandoned; struck down, but not destroyed; hard-pressed on every side, but not crushed. That is the paradox. It looks bad, but there is a way out.

Process

Verses 10 through 13 remind us that it's a process. All four of these stages we have studied are what are called present passive participles. A present tense in the original language meant continuous action. They come relentlessly. Those problems don't only come in your sophomore year just when you are a teen. They don't only come in the middle years of life, or only in your fifties, or your seventies. They keep occurring. They are passive; they come to us regardless. I was driving and moving along when a car passed me—a little pickup truck going about 85 miles an hour as it wove in and out of traffic. Now, if the driver of that car had an accident, he would have no right to look up to God and say, "Why did you do that to me?" We reap what we sow. But this text is reminding us that there are things we don't bring on ourselves—they just come, uninvited. It is the nature of life itself. The trials will come, the tests will come, and if you don't have any I can remind you of a few, if your memory fails. They come, and they keep coming.

In the middle of all of this there is hope. Notice that verses 10, 11, and 12 all talk about life. We are always carrying around the body of the death of Jesus, but the life of Jesus is also being revealed in our body. Verse 11 says, "so that his life may be revealed in our mortal body . . . life is at work in you." Here is the picture: We have the trials, the tests, and the fellowship of His sufferings, but we also have His life, His hope, and His victory. In this life we experience some of His death and in our death we experience all of His life. So don't give up.

The Triumph of Faith

We have been talking about trials; now here is the triumph. We have three tenses of faith: past tense, where we look back; present tense, where we can look up; and future tense, where we can look forward.

Faith in the Past

Verses 13 and 14 deal with the past tense. "It is written: 'I believed; therefore I have spoken.'" So can we with that same spirit of faith believe and therefore speak, "because we know that the one who raised the Lord Jesus from the dead will also raise us with Jesus and present us with you in his presence." Paul is saying one day Jesus got the victory. He was resurrected. We place our faith in His victorious act.

Rudolf Bultman, a German theologian who influenced a number of theologians a couple of decades ago, said we must demythologize the New Testament. He said the mind set in the scientific world calls for the New Testament to undergo a transformation in terms of our understanding. It will not pass the test for modern intellectuals. Therefore, we must go back to the New Testament and realize that part of it is pre-scientific and you demythologize it. One of the ways we do that, he said, which I think is very destructive, is to dismiss the idea of actual historical events. The important thing is that you experience them in your heart. It really doesn't matter if the tomb was empty, or if Christ was resurrected. The important thing is, He is alive in your heart.

Now, that is a very vicious problem, because, if in fact He was not resurrected, and He is only resurrected in your heart, then your heart is deceived. For you have built upon subjectivity and not objective truth. We can never divorce faith from history. If our faith is placed in that which never happened, we have an invalid faith. And faith must also be built upon the foundation of historical data— that which truly happened. He was resurrected—believe it. If Christ was not actually resurrected we have no faith. I was at a banquet where the invocation was brought by Dr. S. M. Lockridge. In his prayer he said, "Lord, we've been back to Calvary, and we've been redeemed. And we've been back to the empty tomb, and it's been affirmed. And we are on our way to Pentecost to experience His power." That is what Paul is saying. We've been back there—it's true—believe it! Our faith is placed in historical data, we can count on it!

Faith for the Present

Our faith has a present tense. "Therefore we do not lose heart. Though outwardly we are wasting away, yet inwardly we are being renewed day by day" (v. 16). We all lose heart. There are days when we are so discouraged and we think this day will never end. Will the trials ever end? Trials always have relatives that keep following after them. Is there no letup in this whole thing? Paul tells us not to lose heart; outwardly we are having troubles, but inwardly we are being renewed. The word "renewed" means taking something that is just barely moving and making it vital and alive again—taking that which is there and functioning inadequately and restoring it to its full usefulness. He is saying that God, by His Spirit, is renewing you within. Outwardly the body may be crumbling—the container, the vial you live in, may not be doing terribly well—but you are being renewed within. That is the confidence we have. We look back, our faith begins there, then inwardly our faith is increasing as we are being renewed. Now he says look forward.

Faith Regarding the Future

"For our light and momentary troubles are achieving for us an eternal glory that far outweighs them all. So we fix our eyes not on what is seen, but on what is unseen. For what is seen is temporary, but what is unseen is eternal" (vv. 17, 18). One of the things the devil does to us is to give us myopic tendencies, and as we look at the problem our whole world becomes so small, and our need looms large and we think all is bleak, and all is hopeless, and all is depressing. Paul cries, "Lift up your eyes and refocus. I want you to get the big picture." Have you ever had someone say, look at this, for in the distance they see a marvelous sight? When the glasses are handed to you and you look through the lenses the view is all blurred. By turning the center knob you can readjust it, and all of a sudden the view becomes clear. It was mind-boggling and beautiful. But you had to refocus. A lot of people have life out of focus. Paul says when we get the big picture and we look down, we will discover in the light of eternity that today can be handled and the problems and trials are nothing compared to what is coming. Refocus—set your faith upon the past, what He has done; the present, what He is doing; and the future, what He is going to do. Then we can handle the tests of life. They will come, but His grace is sufficient. Believe in Him; He is at work right now.

Charlotte Elliott penned a lovely little chorus some years ago called *Just As I Am*. Dr. Charles Elliott, her dad, had a guest at their home, and during the meal he turned to Charlotte and said, "Charlotte, what about your faith in Jesus Christ?" She was offended by the question and said, "I don't want to discuss it," and left. After days of turmoil, she sought out their dinner guest and told him that she wanted to get right with God, but didn't know how. He said, "Come just as you are." So she did. Then she wrote, "Just as I am, without one plea, but that thy blood was shed for me, oh, lamb of God I come, I come."

That is faith at its simplest; that is faith at its inception. Just as you are. You come this way as you enter into the life of Christ, the new life, being born anew by the Spirit of God. This is essentially the way you come when you need to be renewed and restored. I don't know how you are feeling, fellow earthenware jar, but remember we that have the treasure of the gospel in us. We may be fragile, but we have the great power of God available to make us new. Would you trust Him to restore, to renew, or maybe for the first time, to bring you to new life?

Questions for Discussion

1. When have you felt like Paul did—hard-pressed, perplexed, persecuted, and struck-down? Have you looked to God for the way out?

2. Which events from the past strengthen your faith?

3. Is your faith active in the present tense? Are you experiencing the inner renewal that comes from reliance on the Spirit?

4. As you look to the future, is your faith strengthened?

5

That's Why We Are Here!
2 Corinthians 5:11—6:2

"Since, then, we know what it is to fear the Lord, we try to persuade men. What we are is plain to God, and I hope it is also plain to your conscience. We are not trying to commend ourselves to you again, but are giving you an opportunity to take pride in us, so that you can answer those who take pride in what is seen rather than in what is in the heart. If we are out of our mind, it is for the sake of God; if we are in our right mind, it is for you. For Christ's love compels us, because we are convinced that one died for all, and therefore all died. And he died for all, that those who live should no longer live for themselves but for him who died for them and was raised again.

"So from now on we regard no one from a worldly point of view. Though we once regarded Christ in this way, we do so no longer. Therefore, if anyone is in Christ, he is a new creation; the old has gone, the new has come!

All this is from God, who reconciled us to himself through Christ and gave us the ministry of reconciliation: that God was reconciling the world to himself in Christ, not counting men's sins against them. And he has committed to us the message of reconciliation. We are therefore Christ's ambassadors, as though God were making his appeal through us. We implore you on Christ's behalf: Be reconciled to God. God made him who had no sin to be sin for us, so that in him we might become the righteousness of God.

"As God's fellow workers we urge you not to receive God's grace in vain. For he says,

"'In the time of my favor I heard you, and in the day of salvation I helped you.' I tell you, now is the time of God's favor, now is the day of salvation.'"

Have you ever asked yourself the question, What right does the church have to exist as an institution? Does the church have a right to make a claim upon our lives, and ask for a commitment of our energies, talents, resources, to help maintain facilities and programs, and to involve us in teaching, counseling, and sharing through ministry, music, and a variety of other ways? Paul has the answer. God has called us to share a life-changing message that God was in Christ, reconciling the world to Himself. That is why the church exists. We are called to share this message with the world and to build it into our own community. This is the reason and purpose for our very life. It is our manifesto regarding evangelism—the good news which is the gospel. What does this manifesto involve? Our text notes certain things.

———————— **Motivation for Evangelism** ————————

What is it that motivates a person? We have met people who share the Lord quickly and easily, and we ask what moves them to do that? Why do they do it so well and I shrink back? The text reminds us of at least two possibilities: one negative and one positive.

Negatively—Fear of the Lord

Notice verse 11, "Since, then, we know what it is to fear the Lord, we try to persuade men." Everybody has fears. Some have fear of heights, some of being in tight places, others have fear of the unknown, while others have a fear of impending doom. No one is without some fear. The text suggests we ought to have the fear of the Lord. Now we have to be careful that we don't equate this with the fears mentioned above. This fear is not that. This is the fear that belongs to people who have awe and reverence in relationship to the Lord. It is the respect of a person who knows the Master, knows Him well, and wants to serve Him well. Think of a young man who is told by his dad, "Son, today is Monday. I will be away until Friday night. Here are the chores that need doing. Please have them done when I return." The week passes. It is now Friday and tonight his dad is coming home. There's a sense of accountability for the work, and also a sense of expectation—what will Dad think of my work? It is that picture here. It is a picture of people who are sons and daughters of God, who anticipate that someday we shall stand before Him in judgment. Not the judgment of heaven or hell but the judgment referred to in 1 Corinthians 3 which talks about the believer standing before God and whose life is represented either by wood, hay, or stubble; or gold, silver, and precious stones. We will stand before

God to give an accounting of what we have done; whether or not we have been faithful in our service. Paul is saying because someday we shall stand before Him, we need to have that kind of awe that will motivate us. The fear of the Lord is a negative motivator, but a necessary one. There is also a positive one.

Positively—Love of the Lord

There is the love of the Lord on the positive side. See verse 14: "For Christ's love compels us . . . . " This is not our love for Him, but it is His love for us. It is the kind of love that sent Him to the cross—the same kind of love He has for us that compels us, impels us, and propels us to share Him. Love makes us do lots of things, and do it joyfully, without hesitation. Love blesses everything it touches. Thus, if our negative motivation is fear or awe of the Lord, and His love impels us positively, we are then called to respond in obedience. When our family was back in Minneapolis for my son's graduation, we had the privilege of hearing Chuck Colson speak. His life relates to this text. Colson said, "Our goal in life is not to be successful, but to be obedient to Jesus Christ." He indicated his noteworthy achievements in public life: he was a very successful attorney who argued and won several cases before the Supreme Court. He had an outstanding record in political life, and he was a personal advisor to President Nixon. He said, "I was powerful, but do you know what Jesus Christ has chosen to use in my life? My biggest failure: nine months in jail. What does that tell you? Maybe Christ doesn't want to honor my successes, but He wants to humble me and use my obedience." Today, as Colson goes around the country, he is a man who speaks out of weakness. He has discovered that obedience is what the Lord honors. Is there not a parallel in terms of the whole ministry of reconciliation and evangelism? Jesus is seeking our obedience to both the fear of the Lord and His love for us.

———————— Message of Evangelism ————————

"If anyone is in Christ, he is a new creation" (v. 17). Not simply a new creature but a new creation. The word "creation" here is the same word used for creation in the book of Genesis—a word which suggests He makes a new thing. He makes you a new person. The old is past. At the point you received Jesus Christ the old stopped and the new began. The new is continuing, it is ongoing, and God is at work making us new people with new values, new directions for our lives, new interests, sometimes new friends, and a new destiny. That is the message of the gospel.

Reconciled

Notice verse 18, "All this is from God, who reconciled us to himself through Christ and gave us the ministry of reconciliation." The word "reconciled" refers to a specific point in time, once and for all. The minute you trusted Jesus Christ you were reconciled. The war was over. There was peace. Reconciliation takes those who are far apart, who have nothing to do with each other, and brings them together. Picture President Reagan and Fidel Castro as best friends. That is a miracle of God's grace. Now, God is the reconciler. He is the one who takes the initiative. He doesn't have to be reconciled, but He does it. We need to be reconciled—to Him, and so He takes the initiative to make it happen. We become His friends. It happened to John Wesley. You may recall when Wesley came to the United States, he came over as a missionary and then discovered that he was not a Christian. That is an eye-opening discovery for a missionary to come with a message only to discover he has not even experienced it.

Then Wesley went back to England and at Aldersgate he met God in a new way and his heart was strangely warmed. Wesley would say, "That day, I was reconciled. I was at a distance, now brought near." We are reconciled and that is the message that we share.

Righteous

We are not only reconciled, we become righteous. "God made him who had no sin to be sin for us, so that in him we might become the righteousness of God" (v. 21). I don't think there is any verse in the Word of God that more clearly spells out what it is to be justified—that He who was without sin gave us His righteousness, and we who were sinners turned over sin to Him and He gave us His righteousness. It is a picture of judicial giving and receiving. We stand completely guilty before the bar of God. God the Holy Judge looks upon us, but because Jesus Christ has imputed, put in us, given to us, made us righteous, we stand before God as if we had never committed a sin in our lives.

Now, it's interesting to note the text does not say that He became a sinner for us. It says He was made to be sin. I think that is an important distinction. It required a sinless sacrifice to pay the price for sinful people like ourselves; therefore, if He had become a sinner, He would only pay for Himself. But because He was only made to be sin, He stood as the righteous one and took our sin. It's tough to find a parallel for that. Take one who stands completely innocent, standing by you who are completely guilty and he exchanges his innocence for your guilt. He takes your guilt and he suffers all the penalty and the judgment for that sin. This is justification. Jesus Christ is made to be sin. He takes upon Himself our total judgment and pays the penalty, then gives to us His righteousness. We are now justified. Totally guilty people stand innocent before

God because a totally innocent One stood before God accepting our guilt. He was made to be sin for us so that we could be righteous. That's incredible! We are reconciled. We have been apart and we are now brought close. We who are completely guilty are now innocent. That is the message of the gospel. There are people who are far from God who need to know that they can be brought into the very family of God. There are folks who know nothing of righteousness who can become totally righteous. That is the message of evangelism.

Look further in the text. It talks about those who are the messengers of reconciliation. You would think He would have chosen angels for such a great assignment. I mean, when you have got a message like that, when you have a message that says you can be reconciled and you can be righteous, who would you turn that job over to? Angels? No. His first choice was us, not angels. He chose us before the foundation of the earth to be His people and to share it.

———— Messengers of the Good News ————

There are two things I want to say about the messengers of the good news.

Satisfied Customers

First of all they are satisfied customers. Verse 18 puts it this way: "All this is from God, who reconciled us to himself through Christ and gave us the ministry of reconciliation." Paul, the apostles, pastors, all Christians—us! The reconciled. We who have experienced it are to share it. Now that makes sense. We cannot share what we have not experienced. There is a very sobering section in Richard Baxter's classic work, *The Reformed Pastor*, in which he says you cannot be redeemed by a life of sharing the gospel. God will not grant you His life because you have given life to others. You must experience it first of all. You cannot share what you do not have. And those who best share it are those who have both experienced and rejoiced in it. Sometimes we may hesitate to share because there might not be enough change in our lives for others to see a difference, or we are not certain others would want to hear what we have to say. Perhaps. But the text suggests it needs to be shared by those who have experienced it. The best evangelistic sharing does not come out of compulsive guilt—like the lady who made a New Year's resolution to be good to somebody each day. So she did a kind deed for us. When we thanked her she said, "Well, I've got to do a deed a day." We just felt, well, there goes the blessing out of that. We are on her checklist. If you only share the Lord out of guilt because you are going to be accountable to Him one day, that may not be the best way to do it either. The gospel is best shared out of the life that simply overflows. Not where it is tacked on as an item on a "to do" list, and so you look for the first likely person who looks like a non-Christian, and you try to win him or her to Christ. Instead, it ought to flow very naturally out of the relationship of life, work, school, and neighborhood. We do it simply because we have experienced it and we are satisfied customers. Those who share it best are those who have experienced it and have been changed.

Colson made the comment that after he became a Christian he kept a lot of cartoonists in business. You know the cartoons, ones that mocked his conversion to Christianity, and hinted perhaps it might even lighten his jail sentence. He was guilty and so all of a sudden he became a Christian. After the first year the cartoons died off and people began to listen to him. His life had been changed and he had earned credibility. Colson is a man who lives what he shares. That's what the text is talking about. Who are the messengers? Satisfied customers.

The King's Representatives

The second thing the text reminds us is: "We are therefore Christ's ambassadors" (v. 20). An ambassador is both a messenger and a representative—a messenger in the sense that you come along and share, "This is what I received, here is my good news." But more than a messenger, you are a representative. When you speak, you speak on His behalf. When you live before people, you are there as the King's kid. The King's representative. Remember ambassadors are always people in a foreign country, not in their own homeland. I think that is appropriate because if we begin to think this world is our home, it weakens our message. We may be around for 70 or 80 years, but we are just traveling through and our citizenship is in heaven. We are strangers, pilgrims, and ambassadors here, and we are not in our country. We are sent to this country for the sake of the other country: heaven. We are here on earth to represent our Lord. The second thing to remember is that not only are we in a foreign country but we are also responsible for the honor of the other country. Our behavior and example will affect the image of the other land and the God we represent. Ambassadors are chosen carefully, not only for their sense of commitment to their homeland, but also because they are spokespeople for their country. We are the King's representatives. We are to be satisfied customers.

——————— The Method of Evangelism ———————

We have looked at the message; now we need to examine the method. What is the best way to get the message across? Our text tells us in verses 11 and 20. Verse 11 says, "Since, then, we know what it is to fear the Lord, we try to persuade men." There are soul winners—those who are winning people to Christ—and there are soul losers. The difference is often methodology. The text suggests two methods: we do it wisely and we do it urgently.

We are to be wise. Paul calls us to be considerate as we present the gospel, to induce others through the art of persuasion and argumentation in a positive sense. That is what the word "wisely" implies. We use our best abilities to do it well. This text is perhaps an endorsement for evangelistic training, and an encouragement to learn how to share Christ, how to minister with confidence because we know the truth. We know how to share the truth and to do it wisely. Several years ago we were trying to sell a home in the Los Angeles area. We thought anyone who even smiled when driving by our house were potential buyers. We had two Jehovah's Witnesses stop by who indicated an interest in our home since Kingdom Hall was just about two blocks away. And so, one night, not having heard from them and feeling a little desperate about the whole thing, I decided to go to Kingdom Hall to find them. I did not know they had four or five different groups and they each came a different night of the week for training. I entered and found I was in the back of Kingdom Hall. I could not see their faces and I was not too sure I would remember them by the backs of their heads, so I stayed through the training session. They covered everything: what to say to people door-to-door; what to say when the person tells you that there is a Holy Spirit who works in the lives of people, that there is a hell to shun, that Jesus Christ is truly God and equal with Jehovah. The teacher up in front was giving them responses and they were writing and looking up passages in their Bibles. They had what I call the deductive approach to Bible study. That is where you get your theory and then find a verse to proof-text it. Nothing is left to chance. People are prepared with the right word and the right response. They work at it. No wonder they have people responding. They are well-trained, they are active, and they work wisely within their system. We need that kind of commitment—the kind of commitment that would say, Lord help me do it well. Then when we have a course in evangelism, we say, Here am I, teach me, I need all the help I can get. How do you minister to one who is a Mormon? How do you minister to one who is Jewish and does not believe in the New Testament? How do you witness to one who has made a commitment, then becomes an agnostic? "We persuade men," says Paul, which suggests that we use all of the best tools we have for sharing.

Urgency

Paul says, "We implore you on Christ's behalf: Be reconciled to God" (v. 20). I like that. Here is a sense of urgency and compassion. There are certain things that drain us of urgency in our lives. Consider the following.

Insipid universalisms. We would not say on a questionnaire that everybody will be saved, but somehow or other we are not totally convinced all the people we work with, unless they have received Jesus Christ, are bound for hell. So we have a subtle form—a modified form—of practical universalism. We really are not convinced. If you were convinced that every relative of yours, every neighbor of yours, outside of Jesus Christ, was on their way straight to hell, you would probably change. So we have a modified form of universalism.

Churchianity. I can get in trouble with this one. We can become so involved in the life of the church that we do not know anybody who is a real live non-Christian. We don't know anybody very well. We have been Christians long enough so when we go shopping, we go quickly, and we do not look at anybody or speak to anyone unless it is someone we know—usually another Christian. Then we go back home. We may work in the Christian sub-culture. Then we come to church and it feels comfortable because everyone is speaking our language. The longer we know the Lord the fewer non-Christians are in our lives. One of the things we all need to cultivate is the friendship of our neighbors. Those who are beautiful, lovely pagans, but are outside of Jesus Christ. We can get so involved in the work of the church that we forget the work of the church is to reach the world.

The fortress mentality which simply states our main task is to make sure we are right. We are the self-appointed guardians of orthodoxy. As long as our theology is correct and we can define it and we are certain it is pure, and we can defend it, then we can sit back complacently. We forget truth is to be truth lived, truth experienced, and truth communicated. Paul says do it wisely, and do it with compassion and urgency.

When? Did you notice verse 2 of chapter 6? "I tell you, now is the time of God's favor, now is the day of salvation." We forget that death comes suddenly and unexpectedly. A seminary professor gained a little extra weight and decided to take up tennis. While he was playing tennis with his Sunday School class, he dropped dead.

When we were back in the Midwest we were shocked to discover that one of our missionaries, while there for the festivities of graduation, was in a car accident and immediately she and another woman were ushered into the presence of God. Life is so tenuous. We never know. Now, these were godly people, but all around us are people who live just as close to eternity, and yet we lose our sense of urgency. I do not know how much longer we have until the Lord returns, or when people will die, but we ought to be propelled by the love of Jesus Christ so that we share very naturally and compassionately. What a great gospel, what a great message, what a great privilege. Are you sharing it?

Questions for Discussion

1. How well does your life reflect a healthy respect for and fear of the Lord? Does this fear motivate you to service?

2. How well do you remember the day when you were reconciled to God? Have you shared that experience with others lately?

3. Are you a satisfied customer? Are you spreading God's message by word of mouth?

4. Does your life reflect your ambassadorship for Christ? Are you being a true representative?

5. Are you a soul-winner or a soul-loser? How can you improve your presentation of the gospel?

6

A Blizzard of Troubles

2 Corinthians 6:3-10

"We put no stumbling block in anyone's path, so that our ministry will not be discredited. Rather, as servants of God we commend ourselves in every way: in great endurance; in troubles, hardships and distresses; in beatings, imprisonments and riots; in hard work, sleepless nights and hunger; in purity, understanding, patience and kindness; in the Holy Spirit and in sincere love; in truthful speech and in the power of God; with weapons of righteousness in the right hand and in the left; through glory and dishonor, bad report and good report; genuine, yet regarded as imposters; known, yet regarded as unknown; dying and yet we live on; beaten, and yet not killed; sorrowful, yet always rejoicing; poor, yet making many rich; having nothing, and yet possessing everything."

Listen carefully: Becoming a Christian will not solve all your problems. If you're a non-Christian and you have never trusted Christ, you need to know that. Your problems are not all over when you become a Christian. If you are a Christian, you need to be reminded of this. Becoming a Christian will not automatically solve all your problems. In fact, you may pick up a few new ones. You might pick up a problem at work because a new person at the old job sometimes results in conflict. You may pick up some problems at home; change is always traumatic. You may find problems just in being with yourself. New creatures—new people—who are in old settings and in old places with old habits, sometimes create interesting times. That may not only surprise you, it may disappoint you. We may hope the minute that we trust Jesus Christ the problems will be over and it will be clear sailing. But it is not that way. An acquaintance of mine has gone through a blizzard of troubles lately. It has been one thing after another; one trouble leaves and another one comes in the back door, and it has been non-stop. I talked to his wife, and she said "I can't understand it. He is walking with God and he is faithful. He is not selfish, but he is caring and ministering to people. Why this?" That is the bad news. The problems are still here. And they will continue to come, even though we are Christians.

But here is the good news. The big problems are solved—the problem of the past, sin, alienation, separation from God, the heavy burden of guilt. They have been covered. We become not only those who know God, but we become the people of God, the children of God. The distant God now becomes our Holy Father. Then today, when problems come, we have a Friend. We have One who is committed to us, One who will stand by us, who will never leave us and never forsake us. He is there. For the unbeliever the problems are eternal. For the Christian, they are just temporary. We have a future ahead of us. There is a termination date for our problems. They will someday be over in Jesus Christ.

Paul had his problems, and if Paul had his, you and I will have ours. Let us look at his. Read this passage of Scripture from verse 3 through verse 10 and we will discover 28 separate phrases, which cluster into three groupings. The first is verses 4 through 7. And they are in the "in" phrases. In the Greek these phrases occur 18 times between verses 4 and 7. These little phrases are part of the Christian experience. Then Paul has three that are in verse 8; they are called the "by" phrases. These are followed in the latter part of verse 8 through verse 10 by seven paradoxes. There's a little Greek word "as" that notes all seven of these paradoxes. I want to look at just those last seven. The problems that Paul faced, the Lord Jesus faced, the apostles faced, Christians have faced, you and I will face. Let's look at them in order.

Reputation Problems

Paul says, "I am genuine, yet regarded as imposter." That's what we call reputation problems. Try as you may to do your best, people will misunderstand.

Misunderstanding

They misunderstood Jesus, they misunderstood Paul, they misunderstood the apostles, and certainly we're not going to be exempt. We are going to be misunderstood at times, and that will cause immense frustration. We are doing our best, putting forth our best effort, and yet we are misunderstood. Those days do come. It was said of Paul that he was an imposter, which means a deceiver. The people who were false prophets were telling others, "Hey, do you want to know about Paul? He's a fake. He's conning you. He's deceptive, deceitful, and he is leading you astray." That was his reputation, being spread abroad by the false prophets at the church at Corinth. You will have days when people will misunderstand you in the same way, and it will frustrate you. I was recently misunderstood and I felt so bad I just wanted to cry. Have you felt that? If you are human you have. You will face that. You'll be misunderstood. It's part of being a person. People do not always understand. Yet Paul has an encouraging word, "genuine, yet regarded as imposters." Paul is saying the paradox is that people may not understand, but as I stand before God I am genuine. Transparent. True. That is what really matters. That is the final court of appeal. If you are misunderstood by people you have the assurance that before God you are true and transparent. That is all that matters. That's the bottom line. Paul knew that before God he was true, he was genuine.

Popularity

He says "known, and yet regarded as unknown." That's part of reputation, isn't it? People don't know who you are. That's being an unknown, just part of the woodwork. It is like being introduced to an important person for the sixth time and every time it's as if you're meeting for the first time. Unknown. Paul adds, "yet, known, known to God." *The Living Bible* translates it this way: "The world ignores us, but we are known to God." Do you recall the story of the missionary who returned to the United States on the same ship as Teddy Roosevelt. Teddy had been over in Africa on a safari. As the ship came into the New York harbor the band was playing on the pier. It was a festive occasion and everybody was cheering and welcoming back Teddy Roosevelt. The missionary had been overseas for a long time. When he looked down on the pier, he didn't know anybody. Nobody was there to meet him. He had what we all have on occasion—a pity party. His resentful thoughts tumbled through his mind—"I've been serving God; I've been working out there translating the language, giving my life. I've been gone all these years, and nobody cares. Roosevelt's been on a safari, living it up, and he comes back to all this acclaim." Then the gracious Holy Spirit reminded him, "Child of God, you're not home yet." We stand before a God who knows us and considers us important. If you think that you're unknown and you wish your reputation were a little bigger, and you were better known and important people knew you and kept calling you by the right name instead of the wrong name, remember God knows you. We are eternally known to Him.

———————— Physical Problems ————————

Physical problems take two shapes: those which are natural and those which are supernatural.

Natural Ones

"Dying, and yet we live on," would be natural, physical problems. Paul went through that. He was beaten, he was stoned, he was imprisoned, he went through it. He is speaking autobiographically here. Now one of the great frustrations to all of us is that once you trust Jesus Christ your physical problems are not over. The rain falls on the just and the unjust alike. Why is it, we ask, that some people who have walked faithfully with God, have been obedient to Him, have served Him with their lives, in their old age go through such great pain, heartache, and brokenness of body? Why? I don't have easy answers for that. I have asked some of those same questions. I know God is there and God will enable us to handle it, but I still ask, Why? We will not understand this side of glory. I wish we did. Dying, physical pain, and yet, Paul adds, "yet we live on." This is the faithfulness of God. God is there to enable. He's there and we can move on.

Supernatural Ones

Paul adds a phrase, "beaten, and yet not killed." "Beaten" is not a good translation of the original language. Beaten suggests a physical action. It is better translated "chastened." It is that act of a loving God who treats us as a parent; a parent who loves a child very much and therefore disciplines the child. When a child gets out of line it is important to give a pretty strong pat to the north end of the south bound child—to let the kid know that you care enough. The undisciplined child is an unloved child.

Parents understand that. "Whom the Lord loves, He chastens," we read in Hebrews 12:6. It is the ongoing commitment of God to us that says, "Because I love you, I will allow things to come into your life that will continue to move and to shape you into my very image for you." Chastening is part of the process of becoming Christlike. The Apostle adds, "and yet not killed." Job experienced that. He was chastened. God protected him from death but from very little else. But Job came out a better man. We will come out better persons if we allow what God puts into our lives to shape us and mold us. Physical problems will come—expect them. Do not be surprised.

--------------- Emotional Problems ---------------

Second Corinthians 6:10 reminds us there are also emotional problems. Paul says, "sorrowful, yet always rejoicing." The word "sorrowful" can be translated as follows: "grieving, afflicted, doom, depression, melancholy, lamentation." It is Paul's word for saying, "I have bottomed-out emotionally. I have that ache in myself, in my inward being, that won't go away." Mark it well, just because you know Jesus Christ, just because you are obedient, is no guarantee you won't have moments of great discouragement, even depression. That is not a sign of ungodliness. Just as you go to a physician when you have pain and a fever, it may be necessary for you to turn to a Christian friend, a counselor, a psychologist, a psychiatrist, one who can assist you with emotional and mental health. We need that. Those days do come. Paul was there. Some of us have been there, and all of us at one time or another may be there, in emotional hurt and pain.

Then he adds that word that almost sounds ludicrous. "Sorrowful, yet always rejoicing." How do you put those two together? Read the book of Philippians. Here was a church that had those two together. They had gone through trials, testings, difficulties and yet knew great joy. It was the context of their life. God's joy enabled them, even when they were depressed, to know that He was there. Our hearts ache, but at the same time, we have the joy of the Lord. There is no guarantee you won't have emotional problems just because you are a Christian. Finally, here is one that seems to touch all of us on one occasion or another.

Financial Problems

"Poor, yet making many rich; having nothing, and yet possessing everything" (v. 10). The word "poor" means "without"—being empty, penniless, a pauper. I've been reading the biography of John Wooden, UCLA's great basketball coach.[1] He was planning to marry a young lady named Nelly. They had worked hard, put aside money, and finally had $900 in the bank. In those days, that was a lot of money. Today that pays the photographer. But then it could provide a very nice wedding. They went down to the bank to take out the $900 and discovered the bank had gone bankrupt. They had lost it all. John and Nelly had to postpone their wedding. They were so discouraged and they felt terrible. He had been working hard, playing basketball and doing some coaching and all kinds of jobs, and finally saved that money, and now it was all gone. Wooden goes on to say, and I don't know if he said this then as he does now:

"It is one thing for you to lose everything when you are young; you can start again," as they did. "But," he said, "there were a lot of folks in that little midwestern town in their retirement years, or nearing retirement, who had put everything into that bank, and now it was all gone!" That big word, BANKRUPT, can eat away at you like cancer. That pain that comes when all that you have built and all that you have set aside is gone.

Let me add a note of caution here. Please be careful about how you tell people what God is teaching them through their experience. Let them discover that. You probably are not God's servant to identify lessons for God's people. You can be God's servant to listen and to pray with them, but let them discover their own lessons. It is poor timing to say to a person right at the bottom, "Isn't God teaching you some marvelous things?" You are like Job's three friends. Those who stand at the end of the bed and say, "I know someone who died from your problem." Wonderful folks. They're the ones that the hospital limits their visits.

Paul adds the word, "poor, yet making many rich," and that means spiritually rich. Even in poverty Paul was giving people something that neither moth nor rust could destroy. He was presenting them with the riches of life in Christ. Then he goes on to say, "having nothing, and yet possessing everything." Having nothing is being destitute—owning nothing, leaving everything. Yet he adds, "but I have everything. Everything that really matters, I am forgiven. I have a great future. I am a child of God. I have everything that really matters." Does your heart go out to the folks who have gone through terrible winter storms? Perhaps you have personally experienced them. If you have lived through tornadoes you have seen homes destroyed. In a quick flash everything you own is gone and you come out of the southwest corner of your basement, and there is a foundation left, but nothing else. These can remind us to ask the question, What really matters in my life? We have to hold things with a loose rein. There is no permanency built into things. I trust that financial problems don't destroy you; you possess everything that really matters. That is what Paul is saying. I have life in Christ, a great future; my past is forgiven, I'm His, I have you, the people of God. I have everything that really matters.

As you look at a text like this it seems Paul really had some difficult days. But if you look at the lives of people around you, you will discover all of us have our share. We will face difficulties and problems and I trust that you know the Saviour. I don't know what people do without Him. What happens if you discover you have cancer and you don't know Jesus? What happens when you go bankrupt and you don't have the Saviour? What happens when physical illness comes or emotional stress comes if you don't have Christ? Some have said the Christian faith is a crutch—of course it is, because everybody is a cripple! We all have problems. We need Him and He has provided for us. Remember His Word in 1 Corinthians 10:13—"No temptation has seized you except what is common to man. And God is faithful; he will not let you be tempted beyond what you can bear. But when you are tempted, he will also provide a way out so that you can stand up under it." In Christ, we can do it. We can face whatever the world, the flesh, the devil, and life itself brings against us. We will all have troubles. But at times like these we need the Saviour.

Note
1. John Wooden, *They Call Me Coach* (Waco: Word Books, 1973).

Questions for Discussion

1. When was the last time your reputation was called into question? How did you respond?

2. Are you genuine before God? Is your life transparent before Him?

3. What is the toughest problem you face today? Does it involve your reputation, physical health, emotions, or finances? How do you think Paul would encourage you today?

4. What really matters in your life? Do your words and actions demonstrate the priorities in your life?

7

Does God Expect Us to Be Peculiar?
2 Corinthians 6:14—7:1

"Do not be yoked together with unbelievers. For what do righteousness and wickedness have in common? Or what fellowship can light have with darkness? What harmony is there between Christ and Belial? What does a believer have in common with an unbeliever? What agreement is there between the temple of God and idols? For we are the temple of the living God. As God has said: 'I will live with them and walk among them, and I will be their God, and they will be my people.'

"'Therefore come out from them and be separate, says the Lord. Touch no unclean thing, and I will receive you. I will be a Father to you, and you will be my sons and daughters, says the Lord Almighty.'

"Since we have these promises, dear
friends, let us purify ourselves from everything
that contaminates body and spirit, perfecting
holiness out of reverence for God."

Well-meaning Christians across the years have done
some strange things. There was a certain Simon Stylite
who lived on a platform on top of a pillar, 30 to 40 feet
above earth, in order to keep his life clean so he would not
be polluted by the world around him. In the Middle Ages
when the monastic movement was at its height, whole
communities went inward to deny themselves contact with
the unclean world around them. They lived independently,
shut up into their own communities. This has also happened in our own time. Groups have chosen to live a
monastic existence. They have grown their own food,
raised their own chickens, made their own clothes, and in
every way possible shut themselves off from the world
around them to become pure and clean. You are perhaps
aware there are fellow Christians who have chosen not to
be associated with Billy Graham; Campus Crusade; Inter-
Varsity; Young Life; Youth for Christ; or Child Evangelism. The one thing all of these groups have in common is
that they claim their authority from this text.

On occasion I have run across non-Christians with
whom I have shared the Christian faith. They are
impressed by the faith but somewhat unimpressed by
Christians. I recall one person saying, "It all sounds good,
but the Christians I know are weird, and they cause pain."
If we are different because of the gospel, that is OK. But,
if our actions are considered bizarre in the name of Christianity, then that is sad. For you see, we are in this
together. When another Christian hurts, we hurt. When
another Christian rejoices, we rejoice. When the world
thinks Christians are weird, they think we're weird. Let us
look at this text and see what the Word of God is saying.

——————————— **Principle** ———————————

Is the Word of God calling us to be a peculiar people in a strange sense? What does our text really say? Take a look at it. It is so basic to our understanding. Notice verse 14, which states the principle, "Do not be yoked together with unbelievers." "Yoked together" here is a verb that appears no where else in the Word of God. But the adjective, *heterozuges* from which we get this verb, occurs at least two times in the Old Testament. It comes from a word that we know, "heterogeneous" meaning different. Note the two places. Leviticus 19:19 talks about the union of different types of beasts who are really different from each other and yet called to work together, or in Deuteronomy 22:10. "Do not plow with an ox and a donkey yoked together." They are two animals that are very different and they will go in separate directions. The application then, is to the spiritual life. Having a double yoke or double harness calls for putting two together who are going the same direction. We have here a context that helps us understand. Notice 2 Corinthians 6:13, "As a fair exchange—I speak as to my children—open wide your hearts also." In the Old Testament "open wide your hearts" was a bad expression. Deuteronomy 11:16 says, "Be careful, or you will be enticed to turn away and worship other gods and bow down to them." There was always the tendency to tolerate the worship of other gods than Jehovah God, and there was the potential risk of becoming contaminated by idol worship.

Paul says open wide your hearts now, but keep your lives clean. Don't be contaminated. Stop becoming unequally united with unbelievers. As you go to the end of this passage, and the first verse of the seventh chapter, notice that it calls for living a holy life. Don't align yourself with anyone who will bring you down, the text says. Don't align yourself intimately and in an ongoing fashion with anybody who will destroy your spiritual life.

——————————— Problem ———————————

Paul asks five rhetorical questions to highlight the problem. Beginning with verse 14, each one is intended to show how incongruous, how unnatural, how unlikely, how unspiritual that kind of a linkage really is.

Partnership. "For what do righteousness and wickedness have in common?" That is, what kind of a partnership do you have with that which is righteous and that which is without the law, and lawless? They have nothing in common. There is no partnership at all.

Fellowship. The second question—"Or what fellowship can light have with darkness?" The word "fellowship" here is *koinonia.* What koinonia can light have with darkness? They are opposites. They just do not fellowship together.

Harmony. Or the third one—"What harmony is there between Christ and Belial?" The word "harmony" is *sumphonesis,* which is a word from which we get our word, "symphony". Two words: sum—together—and phone—voices. Voices together. What those two have when they come together is disharmony. Christ has nothing to do with Satan. Satan has nothing to do with Christ. There is no harmony there.

Participation. The fourth question—"What does a believer have in common with an unbeliever?" That is, how do they share, how do they participate together? They really have so little in common.

Agreement. The fifth one—"What agreement is there between the temple of God and idols?" Their purposes are worlds apart. They are antithetical. The temple of God here is a reference to your body. We are the temple of the living God. What does that temple, the holy sacred place, the shrine of God, have to do with that which praises idols? The word "agreement" used here means to vote together, and be agreed when you vote. To be committed together. This text points out the temple of God and a temple of idols do not cast the same ballot. They are not agreed in what they are committed to.

Paul is saying, there is no partnership, there is no fellowship, there is no harmony, there is no participation, and there is no agreement between that which is away from God and that which belongs to God. There is no harmony between that which is holy and that which is unrighteous. They just do not come together. Now, if that is true, the third thing that we have to ask is, not only what is the principle and the problem, but how do we apply these teachings to our daily lives.

Application

How do we apply this? First, let me suggest what it does not mean.

Community involvement. It does not mean that you have to shut yourself off from your community. Never. This text is not saying, if you are a Christian you run into your house, pull your drapes, and live silently, privately, completely detached from your neighbors. God calls us to be salt, to be light. We can read the judgment in Matthew 25 that says some day we will stand before God and will be judged by whether we have fed the hungry, given a drink to those who are thirsty, clothed those needing clothes, and visited the lonely and those in prison. We are to be there to be involved. This text should never shut you off from being God's people in your community. We are here for the world's sake. Jesus prayed, "My prayer is not that you take them out of the world but that you protect them from the evil one" (John 17:15). So don't let this text tell you, run from your neighborhood, hide from your neighbors. This text doesn't say that at all.

Healthy Business Pursuits. Secondly, this text is not saying that you can't work for a non-Christian. Can you imagine what would happen if you took that seriously? We would have congregations of the unemployed. Many times you will have no idea whether the business you work for is influenced by a Christian or not. The text doesn't say that as Christians we are to only work with and for other Christians.

Sociability. Nor does the text say you should shut yourself off from being sociable with non-Christians. Remember the reputation that Jesus had? He was accused of mixing with publicans, tax collectors and sinners. My dad preferred to call that Republicans and sinners, which kind of tipped his hand a bit. Jesus, by association, shows He was with the people who needed Him. The world needs us. They need us to be there. Don't shut down, or cut off those opportunities to be a healthy and positive Christian influence to others.

If the text does not call for avoiding community involvement, or healthy business pursuits, or being sociable, what does the text mean?

Marriage to a non-Christian. The first thing the text says, and says dramatically and clearly, is marriage between a Christian and a non-Christian is taboo. Commentators and New Testament scholars agree that for a Christian to marry a non-Christian is always outside the will of God. That means if today, as a child of God, you are courting a non-Christian, you are out of the will of God. That means regardless of how lovely she is, how much he turns your very spirit on, and how delightful she is, if she or he is outside of Jesus Christ, the relationship is outside the will of God. Scripture is clear on this point. What fellowship can a Christian and a non-Christian have together in marriage being yoked together in a lifetime commitment? It would be like yoking together two different animals each pulling in a different direction. Paul is emphasizing that this kind of unequal union threatens us spiritually and drags us down.

But listen carefully, the text does *not* say, if you today as a Christian are married to a non-Christian that you bail out. Read 1 Corinthians 7 written by the same man who wrote this, and you'll discover he encourages you if you are married to a non-Christian, to stay in the marriage, as you could bless the non-Christian and be instrumental in his or her life. If he or she chooses to move out that is acceptable, but as the Christian, this is not to be your initiative. But, it is a clear warning to those who are courting, or someday will court. The best marriage is where a man and a woman in Christ join their lives and walk down life together. It is an exciting moment to hear two young people who know and love Jesus Christ, say, "I do," and begin life together in Him. My heart goes out to those who do not have that in common—it can be so destructive to be divided spiritually. One of the four major reasons for divorce in America today is religion. Stay on your guard. It's better to wait, than to rush into a relationship with the wrong person.

Friends. A second thing the text would also stand against is friends who are non-Christians who can drag you down. You can have non-Christian friends, no question about that; but if that intimate alliance of your life with a non-Christian is pulling you down and you are lowering your standards, then that friendship needs to be broken off. The text is calling us to holiness of life, to building a walk with God where we are His people, and we live in His light. If there is any friendship in your life pulling you down and not enabling or building you, then that friendship is too costly. There are friendships that we must have with non-Christians where we can encourage, help, and minister, but if friends are destroying you, then the text would say do not allow a friendship to take you away from God. The text would also remind us if we are in a business where our commitment to business and to our boss requires us to lower our standards and values, it's too high a price to pay. Any alliance, or allegiance, that is spiritually disruptive and destructive needs to be challenged in the light of this text.

God calls us to walk with Him, to enjoy His fellowship, and to enjoy the good things He provides for us. He desires His very best for us, in marriage, in friendship, in business. He calls us to a walk with Him that will enable us to grow in Him. Anything that would prevent this is too high a price to pay. Challenge the validity of these friendships.

Let me ask you. Are you in harness with anyone destroying you spiritually? Is that the direction you want to go? Where are you going? Who do you stand next to? Who builds, instructs, or guides you? Paul says, build those relationships that will build and lift you in Christ. If you are married to a non-Christian, pray that God will demonstrate His love through you. Trust God to enable you to be His special person in a difficult situation. All of us need to look at our lives and our relationships and ask the question, Where are we going? Is the route we are taking getting us where we want to be as people in Christ?

Questions for Discussion

1. How can Christians strike a balance between being personally involved in the lives of people and not being unequally yoked with unbelievers?

2. How would you evaluate your community involvement? Your business pursuits? Your sociability? Are you active in the world without being influenced by it?

3. Are your friendships or business ties with non-believers affecting you negatively? What will you do to avoid being unequally yoked?

4. Where are you going? Is the route you are taking getting you where you want to be as a person in Christ?

8

A Man Whose Presence Was a Comfort
2 Corinthians 7:5-13

"For when we came into Macedonia, this body of ours had no rest, but we were harassed at every turn—conflicts on the outside, fears within. But God, who comforts the downcast, comforted us by the coming of Titus, and not only by his coming but also by the comfort you had given him. He told us about your longing for me, your deep sorrow, your ardent concern for me, so that my joy was greater than ever.

"Even if I caused you sorrow by my letter, I do not regret it. Though I did regret it—I see that my letter hurt you, but only for a little while—yet now I am happy, not because you were made sorry, but because your sorrow led you to repentance. For you became sorrowful as God intended and so were not harmed in any way by us. Godly sorrow brings repentance that leads to salvation and leaves no regret, but worldly sorrow brings death. See what this godly sorrow has produced in you: what earnestness, what eagerness to clear yourselves, what indignation, what alarm, what longing, what concern, what readiness to see justice done. At every point you have proved yourselves to be innocent in this matter. So even though I wrote to you, it was not on account of the one who did the wrong or of the injured party, but rather that before God you could see for yourselves how devoted to us you are. By all this we are encouraged.

"In addition to our own encouragement, we were especially delighted to see how happy Titus was, because his spirit has been refreshed by all of you."

Our text, written approximately 1950 years ago is a text that could have been written today. It is as up-to-date as anything could be. The problems are our problems. The Bible is different from most books. It doesn't get dated. The Bible is always our contemporary. This text is no exception. It lifts up the need in your life and in mine to be comforted, and the way God uses us to meet that need. The text highlights the life of one of Paul's spiritual brothers. Paul, the author of this letter, was a wise man. He decided the best way to strengthen his ministry was to pour his life into others, and then multiply himself through them. Think about the people he discipled—Silas, Mark, Timothy, Trophimus, Tychicus, Aquila, Priscilla, Titus, Luke, and Demas. Only two casualties among the group: One, a part-time casualty, because he came back—John Mark. John Mark had served God well, then dropped out for a time. Later he was faithful in ministry and was restored to usefulness. Demas seems to have dropped out for good. The text is a rather stinging indictment, "Demas has forsaken me, having loved this present world" (2 Tim.

4:10, *NKJV*). It is a reminder that even Paul had a drop-out.

Look at the ministry of the Lord Jesus. Among his 12 disciples, there was a Judas. Could I add a word to parents. Even if you are faithful to God you may have a man like Demas as a son. You may have a child who chooses, in spite of your faithfulness, not to follow God. We are called to be faithful, not to make our children completely successful and godly. They must each respond to God. If all your children are following God—praise Him.

Let us look at Titus, one of Paul's faithful disciples. Titus was a Gentile who came to faith in the Lord Jesus, and was then accepted into the Christian community without being circumcised. Now, that was unusual in that day, and the Jewish Christians in Jerusalem raised questions. They challenged Paul, and Paul answered them in the letter to the Galatians when he said there is no longer a returning to the law, we now stand by faith through grace. We do not need to return to the bondage of the law. Throughout his writings Paul expresses his close friendship and ties with Titus. He also gave him three special tasks of ministry to the churches.

Need for Comfort

Comfort comes from the Greek *paraklēsis*. It is a verb, meaning to stand alongside, to come alongside to comfort, to be an encourager. Used as a verb, it means to comfort; as a noun, it would be the one who comes to comfort. It is the word that is referred to in John 14:16,17 in the noun form for the Holy Spirit—the *paraklētos*. This is *parakleō*, "doing the work of standing alongside, comforting, and encouraging."

Paul weaves this concept through the passage seven times. Verse 4: "I am greatly encouraged," or comforted;

verse 6: "God, who comforts the downcast comforted us"; verse 7: "and not only by his coming but also by the comfort you had given him." In verse 13 he uses it twice: "By all this we are encouraged," or comforted, "in addition to our own encouragement," or comfort. Paul is expressing a strong need for comfort, and we sometimes miss that. Titus is God's comfort to Paul and God Himself comforts Titus. Titus is the comforter, and as this chapter opens, we see why Paul is hurting. Verse 5 says, "For when we came into Macedonia, this body of ours had no rest, but we were harassed at every turn—conflicts on the outside, fears within." Second Corinthians 2:12,13 gives us the setting: "Now when I went to Troas to preach the gospel of Christ and found that the Lord had opened a door for me, I still had no peace of mind, because I did not find my brother Titus there. So I said good-by to them and went on to Macedonia." Paul was seeking Titus. It had been a long time since he sent him to Corinth. He did not find him at Troas, and so he continued his search, traveling to the northwest up in Macedonia. When he got up there he found Titus, and it was good. He felt relieved, comforted, and encouraged.

Paul recalled those days of loneliness and discouragement in verse 5 of 2 Corinthians 7: "When we came into Macedonia, this body of ours had no rest, but we were harassed at every turn—conflicts on the outside, fears within." Some would like to tell us that the "conflicts on the outside" are the things we face with non-Christians, and "fears within" those we face with Christians. This is wrong. Conflicts on the outside refers to tribulations and external experiences. Fears within are fears inside the person. Let us look at those two.

Problems Without

If you ever think things are tough, look at 2 Corinthians 11 and you will see what problems really are. Maybe you ought to carry this text with you on a bad day:

> "Are they servants of Christ? (I am out of my mind to talk like this.) I am more. I have worked much harder, been in prison more frequently, been flogged more severely, and been exposed to death again and again. Five times I received from the Jews the forty lashes minus one. Three times I was beaten with rods, once I was stoned, three times I was shipwrecked, I spent a night and a day in the open sea, I have been constantly on the move. I have been in danger from rivers, in danger from bandits, in danger from my own countrymen, in danger from Gentiles; in danger in the city, in danger in the country, in danger at sea and in danger from false brothers. I have labored and toiled and have often gone without sleep; I have known hunger and thirst and have often gone without food; I have been cold and naked. Besides everything else, I face daily the pressure of my concern for all the churches" (2 Cor. 11:23-28).

Paul is trying to tell us he has had trouble, and it has been heavy and relentless. That is the wording of 2 Corinthians 7. There is no rest. The word suggests an increasing pressure, with lots of tension and no relief available. It just keeps coming. And Paul groans, "If it isn't jail, it's stoning; if it isn't stoning, it's starving and shipwreck." And he has gone through all of this while doing the will of God. He has had problem after problem after problem.

Pain Within

When there is enough pressure on the outside, it

begins to get to you on the inside. It begins to move inward causing deep, unrelenting emotional hurt on the inside. There is no lessening of the tension, there is no relief, and there is no letup. There were basically two reasons for his pain.

Safety of his dear friend Titus. Titus had been gone a long, long time. Paul had sent him to Corinth, and Titus was to come back with the offering for the church of Jerusalem, which left him prey to being robbed and beaten. I am sure Paul had those days where he said, "I wonder if he is still alive?" He had a father's heart. Dads, do you do that? Do you wonder, "Where's my boy?" I recall one night my son was working at a pizza parlor. He was due to finish work at about one o'clock that morning. The time passed, and I knew it was five minutes from the pizza parlor to home. By two o'clock, he hadn't arrived. Three o'clock. I'm wondering, "Where's my boy?" When he still wasn't home by 4 A.M. I decided to call his friend. His buddy answered, "Oh, yes, Steve's here, we've just been having a good time." Then Steve assured me and added, "And, oh, Dad, I wouldn't have expected you to stay up, I thought you'd be asleep and I didn't want to wake you up." There were lots of dads asleep at that hour, and this dad happened to have a boy out there, and was concerned about him. My little old heart was saying, "Where's my boy?" That is the relationship Paul had to Titus. He was saying, "Where is my son?" He was long overdue and he had not shown up yet, and Paul was in pain.

Success of the work in Corinth. The second thing that concerned Paul was his great love for his church at Corinth. He had sent them a message of encouragement and he was wondering how they were going to respond to it, and what they were going to do. His great heart of love was reaching out to them. There is a parallel to this passage. Timothy was sent to the church at Thessalonica and again Paul's parental concern was evident, until a report came back. Timothy says, "Things are going well in Thessalonia," and Paul says, "Wow, doesn't that feel good?" Paul had a big heart for his churches. He was a caring pastor, and father to his churches. And so he was anxious, looking for Titus, and waiting for the report from the church. Those two things laid heavy on his heart.

We never know what emotional pains people are going through. If we would dare share our hearts, we would discover there are lots of pains. We camouflage the hurt within with a smile and a pleasant exterior because we carry heavy burdens. It may be an illness; it may be our vocations; it may be finances; it could be a boy who is far from God today; or a daughter, a mate, or a parent. Most of the time we are unaware of each other's burdens. I'll never forget the shock when I came home one day, years ago, and discovered a tragedy across the street. Our kids had a lovely baby-sitter. She was pleasant, had lots of friends, a real beauty queen in our little community. Yet she was discovered hanging from the rafters in the basement. She had taken her life. We never really know what's going on inside of people. And, in one degree or another, depending upon our situation, we will all have those times. We just need someone to comfort, encourage, and be with us. Paul was going through that. He had a need for comfort, and so do we.

The Nature of Comfort

Now, I want you to continue in the text and you will discover not only the need for comfort that Paul had, and that you and I share, but you'll see the nature of comfort.

God Is the Author

Chapter 7, verse 6 says that God "comforts the downcast." It is the nature of God to move into the lives of people, to come with His peace and His comfort to stand alongside us, to enable us, and lift our burden. That is His nature. I was privileged to hear Pastor Timothy Winter, of Bayview Baptist Church in San Diego, illustrate this from 1 Chronicles 11. Benaiah was one of David's strong men—not one of the three inner circle members, but next in line. One day Benaiah slew a lion in a pit on a snowy day. As Pastor Winter told it, "It's bad enough to fight lions, but in a pit—you'd like him in a big open field so you can put some moves on him—a lion in a pit, on a snowy day. No traction." Then he said, "You know what we often forget? We often forget there was an unseen assistant in the pit. The lion of Judah! The Lord was there." Then he went on to say, "When you go through your pit, the lion of Judah will be there with you." Paul is saying, "When I went through all these shipwrecks, all of these stonings, all of these problems, I had the assurance that the Lord God Himself was a comforter." He is there in the pit with you. He is the author of comfort.

Man Is the Agent

God is the author of comfort but He uses others as His agents. Verse 6 says, "But God, who comforts the downcast, comforted us by the coming of Titus." I'm sure Paul threw his arms around Titus and said, "Titus, you don't know how good it is to see you." You can just see the big tears slopping down Paul's face. God sends people into our lives like Titus, who come to comfort us. They're the agents of God, who is the author of comfort. He comforts us through his people.

The Corinthians were also a means of encouragement

for him. The text goes on, in verse 8, "Even if I caused you sorrow by my letter, I do not regret it. Though I did regret it—I see that my letter hurt you, but only for a little while." There had been trouble in Corinth, so Paul visited them. He was greatly upset and discouraged by what he found there. After returning, he wrote them a forceful letter. Bible scholars call it a "severe letter." After he had written it and sent it off, he had second thoughts, and wished he had not written it. Did you ever have one of those days? You feel so strongly about an issue, you write to your child, or a friend, and let them know exactly what is on your mind. Once you have mailed it though, you would give anything to intercept that mailman.

Paul felt this, but now he no longer regretted sending the letter because he had received word the letter had worked. It had done what Paul intended it to do. Now he had cause to rejoice. The letter had caused sorrow. Verse 10, "Godly sorrow brings repentance that leads to salvation and leaves no regret." It worked. J. Vernon McGee refers to a story his dad tells about a little boat on the Mississippi. The boat had a big whistle, but a little boiler. When the boat went upstream and would blow the whistle, the boat would begin to slide back downstream, because there was not enough power in the little boiler to both blow the whistle and propel the boat. He went on to say, "A lot of people are like that boat. They have a little boiler with a big whistle. There is sorrow for sin and lots of tears, but they are still going backwards. There is no change." The beautiful thing in this text is that their repentance did lead to change. If God comes to work in your life through the challenge of somebody, and you repent, and change your life—it is all worth it! When Paul got that word it was such a comfort.

God comforts us through people but also when we see change in other lives. There's nothing more comforting than to see people move closer to God when you have committed yourself to them.

——————————— The Bottom Line ———————————

The bottom line goes two directions.

To Receive Comfort

Direction number one. Some of us need to learn to open our lives to receive comfort. Have you noticed sometimes when you are going through deep waters, you retreat? Just when you need others the most. When you are going through difficult times, instead of admitting your need, and allowing the Body of Christ to help, you withdraw and refuse to open up. You risk asking for help. We have to be vulnerable. We only grow as we open. I can't help you unless I know you have need, and you can't help me unless you know that I have need. That's why we have to open up our hearts to each other, becoming candidates for care. Paul was a strong man, but he said, "I need you. I'm hurting." I trust that when you go through difficult times, you will let others know. We all have needs, and need each other. We have to be open, and acknowledge our need.

To Give Comfort

The second direction the text would take us is that God may choose to use you as a Titus. He may ask you to be His instrument, to be available to someone who is hurting, and be His agent of encouragement and comfort. How thankful I am to God that He occasionally taps someone on the shoulder and sends them to comfort me. We are all candidates for comfort. It is so good of our Lord to say, "I'm committed to you. When you are hurting, with pressures without and pain within, I want you to know, I'll be

there, and I will use my people to lift and encourage you."
To be comforted—to be a comforter. This is a ministry
God has entrusted to all of us, the people of God.

Questions for Discussion

1. Think of one recent "problem without" in your life. Can
   you respond to this problem as Paul did to his?

2. Think of one recent "pain within" that has marked your
   life. Can you respond to this pain as Paul did to his?

3. Are you in need of comfort today? Will you go to God
   and His Word to receive it?

4. To whom can you minister comfort today? Will you?

9

The Blessing Plan
2 Corinthians 8:1-8; 9:6-11

"Remember this: Whoever sows sparingly will also reap sparingly, and whoever sows generously will also reap generously. Each man should give what he has decided in his heart to give, not reluctantly or under compulsion, for God loves a cheerful giver. And God is able to make all grace abound to you, so that in all things at all times, having all that you need, you will abound in every good work."

God has wonderful plans for your life. He has plans for your eternity, your salvation, your fulfillment, your vocation, and your family. He especially has plans for your blessing; that is what this text is about. Whoever sows a little will reap a little. Whoever sows generously, will reap abundantly. This principle does not always work in the world of finance. There are those who, with small investments, have made large gains. Yet there are those who invest heavily and lose everything. However, in the life of the spirit this is not true. We have the very guarantee of

God Himself: when you give generously of your life and your resources God will abundantly bless. But whoever gives sparingly, gives to the Lord in the spirit of Ebenezer Scrooge—grudgingly, miserly, holding back—will reap accordingly. A generous response to God results in abundant reaping. A spare response brings spare reaping. That's a built-in spiritual guarantee.

The background for this admonition was the church at Jerusalem. The Jerusalem church had gone through tough times. There had been famine, they had slaves in the church, and in addition, there evidently had been some withholding of the gospel. They were told to share it—to go to Judea, Samaria, and the uttermost parts of the earth. Instead, they kept it in Jerusalem. As a result, souls had shriveled, lives had suffered, and there was a lot of hurt. Paul has urged the other churches to remember the poor saints at Jerusalem. He had received a favorable response. The Macedonians had been magnificent in their giving. Paul now writes to the Corinthians, encouraging them to be as generous as the Macedonians had been. Notice the four principles Paul talks about.

Principles of Generosity

We Give Ourselves

First of all, we give ourselves. That's where it starts. We give of ourselves when God has us—that's the important thing. It is far more important that God possess us, not just our possessions. When God possesses you, He has your attention and He has a claim on your life. One of the beautiful things happening in the lives of some people is when they turn their lives over to God. It's hallelujah time! They have moved out of a life that was built around themselves and shutting out God. Now God is the central controlling influence, power, and person in their life, and for the first time life begins to get perspective. "There- fore, I urge you, brothers, in view of God's mercy, to offer your bodies as living sacrifices, holy and pleasing to God— which is your spiritual worship" (Rom. 12:1). That's first. The people responded favorably to Paul's pleading. Notice verse 5 of 2 Corinthians 8, "And they did not do as we expected, but they gave themselves first to the Lord and then to us in keeping with God's will." God wants you more than anything. That's first.

We Stop Calculating

Generosity is not related to wealth at all. You can have everything and not be generous, or you can have precious little and be very generous. It has nothing to do with your bank account; it has to do with your spirit and your atti- tude. When my son Steve was a senior in high school, the pledge reports were sent out at the end of the church year. Steve's card showed he had given $700 plus. He was working part time, at minimum wage, and he had given over $700. I talked to Steve. He said, "Well, I just wanted to do that. I think it is an appropriate thing to do." The Lord had blessed him with two things: a heart that just loved the Lord, and the spiritual gift of not knowing how to make mathematical calculations. He didn't know how to figure 10 percent, and he had given about 33 percent, as I recall. That is a marvelous spiritual gift—when you don't calculate and you can't figure out 10 percent any longer. But when you start to calculate, you become rigid and for- mal. When you get freed up you will do what the Macedo- nians did. Verse 2 of chapter 8, "Out of the most severe trial, their overflowing joy and their extreme poverty welled up in rich generosity." Severe trial and extreme poverty is depression time. It is time to pull in your oars, to feel like the world has turned sour. Yet what is it matched with? They have had a severe trial, so they had overflowing joy. They had extreme poverty, so they gave generously. That doesn't make sense. That doesn't make sense to the natural man, so he says, "I don't believe or understand that." Of course not. If you don't know Jesus that is dumb. If you know Jesus, you say, "Isn't that neat!" To know Him is to have the Spirit release you so that your experience has nothing to do with your generosity. Generosity is an attitude that says, "I no longer calculate, I just do it."

In George Orwell's novel *1984,* the main character begins to separate himself from the totalitarian state and wants to be an individual. One of the things he does is to get a girlfriend, Julia, and he wants to express his love in freedom. The state discovers it, and they want to take that love away from him. So in order to grind him down, they put a mask full of wild, starving rats over his face. He then cries out, "Do it to Julia, do it to Julia." The mask is removed. He is now a successful candidate for faithfulness in a totalitarian state, for he has become selfish and has lost his personhood. Our text reminds us that our greatest reality as persons, our fulfillment as persons, is to be outgoing and share our lives. It will hurt if we only go inward. It will shrivel our souls.

We Fall in Love

"I am not commanding you, but I want to test the sincerity of your love" (8:8). Paul questions their motivation. What motivates you in your relationship to God? What motivates you in relationship to your gifts? What motivates you in relationship to your service? If you're in love with God, you are free to give. The big question is the one asked of Peter, "Peter, do you love me?" When you can answer that in the affirmative, you will have a life of generosity. Love is generous. You'll notice verse 9 of chapter 8 says, "For you know the grace of our Lord Jesus Christ, that though he was rich, yet for your sakes he became poor, so that you through his poverty might become rich." He gave freely, He gave abundantly, and He set the pattern for us. We are called to reciprocate His great love.

We Respond Spontaneously

Look at two verses: chapter 8, verses 3 and 4, "For I testify that they gave as much as they were able, and even beyond their ability. Entirely on their own, they urgently pleaded with us for the privilege of sharing in this service to the saints." Imagine a Monday morning, and you are standing outside your church office, knocking, insisting that even though you gave on Sunday you want to give more today. "Please open up so I can come in and give more." The secretary would have to be revived and given a glass of water to bring her back. Everyone would be overwhelmed. That is the spirit of the Macedonians. They said, "Don't keep it from us; don't deprive us; give us the opportunity to be generous."

Then verse 7 of chapter 9 is the other part of this, "Each man should give what he has decided in his heart to give, not reluctantly or under compulsion, for God loves a cheerful giver." Paul was concerned about two things: one is what he called thoughtless giving. Your giving is prompted by the plate coming down your aisle, and since you wish to appear in a good light, you look for something to put in. The Lord would prefer that we spend time in His Word, spend time with Him, and then give out of a generous response of our heart to God, and in obedience to His leading. Maybe this week you could set time aside to ask the Lord, "What do you want of my life this week? My resources, my talent, my time are all yours." Then your giving is a thoughtful response of a loving heart. The other concern Paul had was unwilling giving. He wanted giving to be spontaneous, not motivated by coercion or guilt.

There are religious groups you can belong to that will assess you, and when you join and become a member they will send you a bill for your initiation fee. Once you are a part of the group, you are sent an annual assessment in the form of a bill. That is what is expected. That runs contrary to everything I understand of the heart responding to God freely and spontaneously. Then our giving is generated by love and it is the reflex of the loving heart. That's the way it ought to be.

—————————— Benefits of Generosity ——————————

When we give generously it benefits God, it benefits others, and it benefits us. That's all. Just God, others, and us. But that's plenty.

God Is Praised

Notice what it says in chapter 9, verse 11 and following, "through us your generosity will result in thanksgiving to God. This service that you perform is not only supplying the needs of God's people but is also overflowing in many expressions of thanks to God." The *glory of God, worshiping God, and praising God* are abstract terms. If the chief end of man is to worship God and enjoy Him forever, how do you worship Him and how do you glorify Him? The first way is to give your life to Him. Then give your resources in generosity. God is thanked and God is praised and glory is brought to God as we respond to Him generously.

Needs Are Met

The church I pastor needs $39,000 a Sunday to meet our budget. But what are we doing with it? There is a lot happening. If you'd come here during the week, you'd almost have to have a traffic policeman. The traffic going in and out of here is unbelievable all the time. It's a busy place! We have 150 plus students in a preschool, about 100 in Southern California Bible College, 111 at Bethel Theological Seminary West; we have an active senior program all day Thursday. A large Bible study meets here on Tuesday. We have over 300 singles that meet every Sunday morning—the largest singles ministry in all of San Diego County. We have 700 university students every Sunday—the second largest college ministry in the United States. We have a busy counseling center ministering to people in a variety of situations. We have 110 plus missionaries across the world that we are supporting. Much happens here and much is going on around the world just because God has touched the hearts of men and women to make that happen. What a privilege. And the privilege that we have is that we choose it as God's people—what God wants us to do. The people of the church I pastor support that. One of the things that's always concerned me about other ministries out there is that you don't know what they are doing with the money—you don't know how it's being spent; you give it but you have no idea how it's spent.

One of the privileges we have as a people of God is to say how we want to use our money to serve God. You determine it, you support it; it is our privilege to do it prayerfully and knowingly, and needs are met. Lots of people around the world depend upon faithful giving from Christians. We are helping support churches all across America and the world that are just beginning and through our gifts we are helping them get along.

We Are Blessed

We get blessed at the same time. Verses 10 and 11 of chapter 9 say He "will enlarge the harvest of your righteousness. You will be made rich in every way." As you begin to give and become generous and allow God to just free you up, it will bless your heart, it will bless your spirit, it will bless your whole life. That is a guarantee of a generous God who has given so abundantly to us. Do you recall the story of John D. Rockefeller? He was a millionaire by the age of 33, and a billionaire by the age of 43. I would assume those were 10 very good years. At 53 he was the richest man in the world. He netted over $1 million dollars a day. That is more than most of us will make in a lifetime. Total! Every day! But he was dying. His soul had shriveled; physically he was going downhill—he could only eat crackers and soft bread and drink milk—and he was dying. Then he discovered if he would open up his hands and share what he had been given, his life would be honored. So he began to give money away and to share. He opened up hospitals, educational institutions, and churches. Many organizations across America enjoy the benefits of that Rockefeller money. When he began to give it away, his health returned and he died at 98. He had learned the secret of generosity. And that happens regardless of how much you own. God honors and blesses open hands and giving hearts that love Him.

The blessing plan. Whoever sows miserly will reap so. Whoever sows abundantly will reap abundantly. Have you tried God's Blessing Plan? It works! It will bless your life; it will bless the world.

Questions for Discussion

1. Have you given yourself completely to God? What is stopping you?

2. Is your generosity a result of careful calculation or of spontaneous and overflowing joy?

3. Does your love for God result in generous giving?

4. What happens to the money you give to the church and other Christian ministries? Do you know how your gifts are being spent?

5. What blessings have you experienced as a direct result of your generosity? Have you thanked God for these blessings?

10

Fight the Good Fight
2 Corinthians 10:1-6

"By the meekness and gentleness of Christ,
I appeal to you—I, Paul, who am 'timid' when
face to face with you, but 'bold' when away! I
beg you that when I come I may not have to be
as bold as I expect to be toward some people
who think that we live by the standards of this
world. For though we live in the world, we do
not wage war as the world does. The weapons
we fight with are not the weapons of the world.
On the contrary, they have divine power to
demolish strongholds. We demolish arguments
and every pretension that sets itself up against
the knowledge of God, and we take captive
every thought to make it obedient to Christ.
And we will be ready to punish every act of disobedience, once your obedience is complete."

Have you ever had a friend who constantly checked
your spiritual temperature? When I lived in Boston I had
such a friend. Whenever I saw him he always asked the

same question, "Dan, have you got the victory?" After a while that got kind of irritating, but I noticed I was doing quite well when he was around, because I knew he would hold me accountable. Now, it's my turn. *Have you got the victory?* You see, it's possible that you do have victory. But it's very possible that you don't. You may be living in defeat. You come to crises and fall, or you come to difficulties and fall. Or you occasionally enjoy the victory, but most of the time, you experience defeat. How's it going? Have you got the victory? Paul knew we would face conflict. He dealt with it in a number of passages in the Word of God. In Romans 7 he talked about the civil war going on inside. He said, "the things I should do, I don't. What I shouldn't do, I do. Oh wretched man that I am. When am I going to get over this?" Or, in the last chapter of Ephesians he talks about taking on the whole armor of God. Why? Battle! We're doing battle.

Paul is now changing the tone of his letter. You will notice as you get to chapter 10 of 2 Corinthians there's a mood change. Chapters 1-9 dealt with a relationship to his friends. There's a spirit of caring, tender compassion, encouragement, and gentleness. But once we move into chapters 10-13 the tone changes. Paul is rebuking his enemies. Here we see him rising up in stern, passionate, severe rebuke. The text deals with the treatment he received from the hands of the Judaizers who were a minority, but were undermining, undercutting, and destroying Paul's ministry. He faces it head-on.

——————— **There's a War Going On** ———————

The thesis of this text is that there is a war going on. Notice verse 3, "For though we live in the world, we do not wage war as the world does." Paul knew about the Roman army; he had watched it in action. He now applies the principle of conflict and the military motif to the Christian life. We are in a battle. We are in an ongoing war. The word "world" appears twice in verse 3 and again in verse 4: "For though we live in the world, we do not wage war as the world does. The weapons we fight with are not the weapons of the world." Perhaps your translation substitutes the word "flesh" for "world" there. It is the Greek word *sarx*. It can be used three ways. It can refer to our body. When the Scripture talks about flesh, it's talking about this body of ours. J. Vernon McGee refers to this word and says it means the meat on our bones. A second usage refers to weakness and the fact that we are in the flesh. That means we are frail—there is no immunity; we are not shut off from all the problems around us. We are not hermetically sealed off from what faces the unbeliever. You have it and I have it.

The third usage is perhaps Paul's most common use of it—the moral sense in which it means the corrupt nature that all of us have. "For I know that in me (that is, in my flesh) nothing good dwells" (Rom. 7:18, *NKJV*). Inside of me, the old nature is warring against the new nature. The minute I trusted Jesus Christ the war started. The old and the new, in conflict.

Harold Ockenga says the Christian life is the Garden of Eden. The first skirmish is in the garden. The Christian life is lived in the garden, and we all fight the battle of Armageddon personally, as some day it will be fought in the Valley of Megiddo. The war is on—in your life and in mine. If you are a Christian, there is conflict. There's a battle.

I want you to note the areas in which we do our battle. The text suggests three.

The emotional battle. The first area is emotional. "By the meekness and gentleness of Christ, I appeal to you— I, Paul, who am 'timid' when face to face with you, but 'bold' when away!" (v. 1). This is what they were saying about Paul. They were saying, "Aha, he's really bold when he's away, but when he gets with you he's timid. He's inconsistent. He's tough when he writes those letters, but in person he's a pussycat." They were attacking his character and his credibility. And one of the great battles we have is what people think about us and our response to that. Have you heard the commercial on the radio where a fellow is rehearsing what he is going to tell the boss about a medical plan that will save them money and benefit the company? "I'm going to go right in there and I'm going to tell him that we need it; it'll save money for the company." He is saying these words to himself as he's on the way to see his boss. The boss says, "Hello, there," and all he can say is, "Hi!" Bold in the hall, timid with the boss. That is what they were saying about Paul. Big deal! Tough guy when he writes letters. Not so hot in person. Paul had to deal with that, and that's an emotional battle—what people feel about you, how they feel about you, what they say about you. I recently read the comments of Howard Hendricks as he voiced disappointments at all those who are leaving the pastorate. Most are leaving because of criticism on the part of congregations and individuals. Hendricks goes on to say that congregations generally have 85 percent who are supportive of their pastor and 15 percent who aren't. The pastors who leave listen to the 15 percent and forget about the 85 percent. And his comment is, "Don't let 15 percent drive you from the ministry." It happens all the time; Paul had about 15 percent who spoke out against him. They challenged him, but they were a minority. And Satan can use these criticisms, these feelings, to destroy you. You don't have to be a pastor to discover that. How people regard you, what they say about you, your response—are all potential arenas for emotional battle.

The intellectual battle. The second battle we fight, in

addition to the emotional, is the intellectual one.

Verse 5 says, "We demolish arguments." The word translated "argument" comes from the same root word as "logic" and can mean speculations or reasonings that have a degree of verifiability; those cognitions that are marshalled together to build a case. These are set against the knowledge of God and the truth of God. It is the battle that goes on in the mind of the believer who fights all the philosophies all the reasons and positions that are a challenge to the truth of God. You can be destroyed by them or defeated by them. I think of the students who come into my office and tell me how professors delight in mocking and ridiculing Christians. One of the things that I've discovered with those professors as I've gotten to know them is that almost without exception they have had a bad experience in Sunday School or with parents who were legalistic. They have never gotten over emotional bitterness, so they take it out on their students by marshalling all of their data—you can select data any way you choose—and using it to lash out against the students. Students fall under the pressure of that philosophical academic attack directed to the intellect. Tragically we see Christians falling by the wayside. Satan can beat us in the mind, and yet historically the greatest minds have been believers, men and women deeply committed to God.

There's another word in the text that gives us a clue. It is that word "pretension"—the idea of being inflated or puffed up; pride. There is something about the intellectual mind that puffs itself up. If you can domesticate ideas, or can define them, you are immune from needing God. You are independent, you can control ideas. The temptation is then to think, who needs God?

I read somewhere that the Victorian agnostic Huxley spent the weekend with a Christian family. Sunday morning, in order to avoid going to church, Huxley asked one of the family members, "Why don't you stay home and you can tell me why you believe in Jesus and why you believe in Christianity?" The response was, "You'd destroy me with your arguments." Huxley said, "No, I don't want to argue with you, I'm just interested. Just tell me why you believe what you do." Encouraged, the gentleman shared while the others went off to church and quietly told him why he had trusted Jesus Christ with his life. When it was done, William Barclay, who tells the story, said tears came down Huxley's face and he said, "I would give my right arm if I could believe that." There is something proud that distances us, making us almost immune to the sweet reasonableness, gentleness, and the ongoing spiritual logic of the Christian faith. Even Christians face those battles for the mind.

The volitional battle. In addition to the emotional and intellectual battles, there is a third one, what I call the volitional battle. "We take captive every thought to make it obedient to Christ" (v. 5). Paul was saying that our thought life is a battleground. What we choose to think about, what runs across our mind, what controls us, what predisposes us to behave in a certain way—all are arenas for conflict. We can choose what we allow ourselves to think. We entertain what we choose, and we can refuse what we want. Ask yourself, what do you let into your mind? That will determine your behavior. Battles go on in our thinking, and this is where too many of us will lose the battle.

I was recently at an outdoor restaurant. Several tables away was an older lady, eating by herself. Periodically she broke off a little bread and tossed it on the ground to a little bird fluttering nearby. The bird came over and enjoyed it; another piece, and a third piece. She slipped over to the buffet to get something, just one item, came back and the bird was in the center of her plate eating her meat and potatoes. Thinking is like that. You can entertain a thought and play with it, but you never know when it's going to come back and destroy you. Be careful what thoughts you entertain. They could overpower you. Therefore, Paul says, we bring "every thought into captivity to the obedience of Christ" (v. 5, *NKJV*). Well, the battles are on, emotionally, intellectually, volitionally, and a number of other ways, but there's also a victory to be won. Paul gives us some clues about that.

——————— There's a Victory to Be Won ———————

Adopt a Proper Attitude

Notice what he says in verse 1 of chapter 10, "By the meekness and gentleness of Christ . . . " He is saying, this is my appeal to you in this environment, in this context. Those two things, "meekness," which is humility, and "gentleness" (or sweet reasonableness) should characterize the environment we do battle in. The character of our Lord, Paul says, should be reflected in us. And when you are in battle, you don't need to be bitter. In gentleness and meekness come humbly before God, saying, "There's a battle to be won, and I come dependently and graciously to you." Come in a proper attitude.

Use the Spiritual Weapons

Secondly, use the spiritual weapons. "The weapons we fight with are not the weapons of the world. On the contrary, they have divine power to demolish strongholds" (v. 4). What has that power? Two weapons—the first is the Word of God; the second, prayer.

The Word of God is called the sword of the Spirit (Eph. 6:17). The text says, we do not wrestle and fight with the weapons of the world, or the flesh. Think about the temptation of Jesus. After 40 days, He was in a weakened condition, and Satan came to Him. What did He use to destroy the onslaught of satanic attack? His rhetoric? No! The power of His presence? No! The wisdom of a keen mind? His charisma? No, He did not use any of those. On each attack He took out the sword and did battle using the Word of God: "It is written" . . . again, again, and again.

He used the sword of the Spirit. And if Jesus did, how foolish of us to think by our own wisdom, using the weapons of this world and of the flesh, we can do battle against the powers of satanic attack. The Word of God is your sword, use it! Unfortunately, a lot of people have a beautiful sword, kept in a beautiful leather sheath, which just sits there while they get destroyed. Whip it out! Do battle!

Prayer is our second weapon. "Pray in the Spirit on all occasions with all kinds of prayers and requests" (Eph. 6:18). Bob Thornburg, a good friend, has been recently in Korea, and he gave me an update on his experience with the Prayer Congress. The Korean church is experiencing such great revival. One church will have 500,000 members within a few years. One church! I'm not sure of the exact numbers, but 25,000 to 30,000 attend five services on Sunday morning, with no parking lot. They come by public transportation. But, why is this Presbyterian church, and churches all over Seoul and across Korea, experiencing great revival? They pray. They go up on the bus to the prayer mountain and pray all the way; pray all day and all night; and pray all the way back. What are they praying about? Bob gave me a clue—they *PRAISE*! Think about your prayer life, or if you prefer, think about my prayer life. How do I pray? I ask the Lord, "Bless my food; watch over my boy; protect my mother; be with my daughter and my wife and my mother-in-law." I've got lots of requirements for God. He keeps busy, because I keep asking—"Help me; forgive me; watch me; guide me; bless them; care for them." But PRAISE! That's a thank offering to God. If you change the whole motif of your prayer from "give me; forgive me; use me; bless me; guide me; direct me; care for me" to "PRAISE HIM" your life will be purified through praise better than all the confession in the world. Here is an assignment. This week, don't ask God for anything, just praise Him. Every time you are tempted to ask Him for something, just praise Him. Don't say thank you for the food, or bless the food, just praise Him for it. Don't ask Him to heal your body this week; just praise Him for the health you've got. Don't ask him to straighten out a relationship you have with people; thank Him for the good ones you have. Just praise Him. You may pray a little less, but you will pray a lot better. Praise Him! Praise purifies! Try it! If you run out of words, pray some of the Psalms back to the Lord. David knew how to praise Him. There is more about praise than prayer in the Bible, yet how few praise meetings there are. Praise Him.

Claim the Available Power

Finally, after adopting the correct attitude, and using the spiritual weapons, we are to claim the available power. "They have divine power to demolish strongholds." The words "demolish strongholds" convey the idea of a battering ram that knocks down a huge building set up against you. Have you ever seen a large downtown building destroyed? That great big ball smashes into the side, leaving just dust and rubble. That picture of a battering ram gives us a reminder that in Jesus Christ, and in the power of the Holy Spirit, you have a divine battering ram that demolishes those things that war against you. When the attack comes you have the power of the Spirit of God.

Back to the first question—HAVE YOU GOT THE VICTORY? You could! "No temptation has seized you except what is common to man. And God is faithful; he will not let you be tempted beyond what you can bear. But when you are tempted, he will also provide a way out so that you can stand up under it" (1 Cor. 10:13). There is victory available, but you must claim it. The battle is on! Have you got the victory? You could!

Questions for Discussion

1. Are you now fighting emotional, intellectual, or volitional battles? What will it take to overcome victoriously? Have you asked God to meet those needs?

2. Are your battles characterized by meekness and gentleness?

3. Have you utilized the weapons available to you—the Word of God and prayer? What has stopped you from doing so?

4. Have you praised God today? Why not do so right now?

11

God's Seal of Approval
2 Corinthians 10:7-18

"You are looking only on the surface of things . . . . For some say, 'His letters are weighty and forceful, but in person he is unimpressive and his speaking amounts to nothing.' Such people should realize that what we are in our letters when we are absent, we will be in our actions when we are present.

"We do not dare to classify or compare ourselves with some who commend themselves. When they measure themselves by themselves and compare themselves with themselves, they are not wise. We, however, will not boast beyond proper limits, but will confine our boasting to the field God has assigned to us, a field that reaches even to you. We are not going too far in our boasting, as would be the case if we had not come to you, for we did get as far as you with the gospel of Christ. Neither do we go beyond our limits by boasting of work done by others. Our hope is that, as your faith continues to grow, our area of activity among you will greatly expand, so that we can preach the gospel in the regions beyond you. For we do not want to boast about work already done in another man's territory. But, 'Let him who boasts boast in the Lord.' For it is not the man who commends himself who is approved, but the man whom the Lord commends."

Some time ago I was at a dinner in another city. As I was seated, I recognized everyone at my table but two. I turned to the one on my left and said, "I don't believe we've met. I'm Dan Baumann and I'm from San Diego." The stranger gave his name, his location, and then he began a five-minute review of his accomplishments—his title, his past history, how he'd moved up the corporate ladder, the number of people that were responsible to him, he even indicated his salary. I was getting embarrassed for him, I looked around, and noticed others were squirming. Then I began to be critical of him. And then it dawned on me I was hearing the same things I've heard my wife's husband say. It made him look so bad, and yet I was beginning to look at myself and say, "Oh my, that's touched home. Maybe there are some lessons to be learned because of the way I feel when they do it, I wonder how people feel when I do that. Not very pleasant." This is PRIDE, the first in the list of the seven deadly sins. Perhaps the most obnoxious sin.

It was pride which caused Satan to fall. In Ezekiel 28:16 it says that his "heart became proud," and in Isaiah he proclaimed, "I will make myself like the Most High" (Isa. 14:14). Pride destroyed him. Go back to the garden, at the beginning of human history with a man and a woman. What caused their fall? In part, it was pride. "You will be like God," Satan said. He held out that tantalizing prospect for them, and they took it. Pride causes a great deal of havoc today. For you see, whenever pride comes, we take God off the throne of our lives and place ourselves there.

Paul addresses the issue of pride as he begins this section. He continues the process that began in verse one with his defense of the ministry. He has been under criticism and is defending his right to be a servant of God. Against the backdrop of what his critics in Corinth are saying about him, he weaves the idea of proper boasting. He shows how pride is a sin and suggests the antidote is praise. Let's look at it.

———————— The Anatomy of Pride ————————

Pride is called, "vain glory" in some translations. As Paul talks about it he says the problem is invalid, inadequate criteria, when you build your case upon something which can't bear the weight of it. The first problem is you build it on externals.

Based on Externals

Paul is saying if you just settle for the externals they are always inadequate. The Greeks did. They placed a great deal of confidence in the way you looked, how you sounded, your title, your performance. The inside wasn't important—forget what your heart is like. It's against that cultural setting that Paul points out that the anatomy of pride is built upon externals which are always inadequate. These include the following.

Beauty. "Some say, 'His letters are weighty and forceful, but in person he is unimpressive'" (v. 10). Physically, Paul did not look good. That's what they were saying. If you put together all that we have from tradition, plus the little clues that Paul drops in his 13 Epistles, you get an idea he was not a handsome man. The *Acts of Paul and Thecla,* the *Writing of Chrysostom,* and one other early writer combine to give us the following picture of Paul: short, bald, wrinkled, thick beard, bow-legged, meeting eyebrows, hooked nose that looked like an eagle. Movie star material he was not. Paul is saying, physically I may not come out as a winner. In Greek culture appearance was one of the bases of your worth. Things haven't changed much. We still have beauty parlors and exercise gyms. Now, I would never encourage people to look tacky, and I'm not sure the text would ever say that. I think that we have a responsibility to be neat, clean, and to look our best. But, if you build your life around your beauty and its external appearance, you have built upon a foundation that can't bear up under the test. It's inadequate. It's pride.

Eloquence. "His speaking amounts to nothing" (v. 10). That was not what you wanted to hear from the Greeks. The Greeks placed a high premium upon the ability to capture ideas and share them in such a way as to move people, to make language your servant, and be able to move people through the power of your rhetoric, eloquence, and oratorical skill. On days when I talk about eloquence, I get a firsthand experience on its inadequacy. I had the invocation in a service, and I couldn't put two sentences together. I started a sentence that was going nowhere, and I was just stumbling over my words. I thought how gracious the Lord is to take our desires and by His Spirit make sense out of them. But I'm not sure what the folks at the service thought. They probably thought, he's still asleep. On the day I talked about eloquence, the Lord reminded me that I can't rest in my ability to articulate. I thought, the Lord has such a wonderful sense of humor, I wished He'd play it on someone else. If you build your worth upon your ability to articulate, and your eloquence, you have built it upon an inadequate criteria.

Accomplishments. Paul doesn't refer much to his accomplishments in this text, but he does throughout the book. He lists all the things that he has done. He talks about righteousness, and he fulfilled it. Legalistically he did the right things. He was zealous. He even went out and captured Christians because he thought it was the right thing to do. And yet, Paul said, it's all dung (see Phil. 3:8). You can't pride yourself in your accomplishments, or your kid's accomplishments, as the case may be. A little while ago, I met with two men who are editors at Multnomah Press, the company publishing Chuck Swindoll's books. One of his recent books, *Seasons of Life,* is now in its fifth printing and has sold somewhere around 250,000 copies. The average Christian book sells 3,000 copies in its lifetime, yet his sold a quarter of a million in less than a year. The editors said, "Chuck Swindoll is not impressed by himself. We work with him; he brings his manuscripts to us, and we work them over. The impressive thing about him is, we tell him how well he is doing and he just laughs about it. He just doesn't take himself seriously. He's just 'plain old Chuck.'" Now I want to read him, even more than before, because here is a man who is not impressed by his accomplishments. A man who recognizes that God gave the gifts, he is just simply using them.

You can't pride yourself on your looks. You can't pride yourself on your eloquence or your accomplishments. They are always inadequate. You're setting yourself up for the ugly sin of pride.

Based on Comparisons

There is another problem that develops. Notice verse 12. (J. Vernon McGee says that "this is Paul's sense of humor coming through.") "We do not dare to classify or compare ourselves with some who commend themselves.

When they measure themselves by themselves and compare themselves with themselves, they are not wise." That is literally, stupid. It is stupid to compare yourself with yourself and with those like yourself. They compared themselves with inadequate people—carnal saints—so that they would look adequate. You can always do that if you want to look good; compare yourselves with those who aren't doing well. But, what you really need to do is compare yourself with those who are walking with God. Or better yet, stand before a holy God and watch your pride disintegrate. What happened to Isaiah? Isaiah was in the temple, the Lord was high and lifted up—"holy, holy, holy." Isaiah doesn't say, "I'm looking good." He says, "Woe is me, I'm undone" (see Isa. 6:5). If you are full of pride, saying, "I performed well, and I'm really moving on," and have an inflated view of your own importance, walk into the presence of our Holy God and you'll recognize how far short we all fall. But if you compare yourself with yourself and with people like yourself, there's no incentive to move on.

Based on Deceit

A third problem Paul explores is deceit. "Neither do we go beyond our limits by boasting of work done by others. Our hope is that, as your faith continues to grow, our area of activity among you will greatly expand, so that we can preach the gospel in the regions beyond you. For we do not want to boast about work already done in another man's territory" (2 Cor. 10:15,16). Paul is saying we don't want to be proud of what someone else accomplished. It is deceitful to take personal credit for someone else's performance. It's probably the same difficulty that arises with second generation wealth. The parents worked hard, spending hours, pouring their lives into it, but they accomplished much financially. And, as the ad puts it, "We make our money the old fashioned way; we earn it." The second generation inherits it, and they're proud. They didn't earn it. Paul is saying, I'm not going to take credit for what someone else did, that's based on deceit. Credit goes to those who earn it.

The classic educational story is the one that arose at a seminary. Seminary students as you know have not been glorified nor completely sanctified. And this story is about one seminarian on his way to sainthood. He had an assignment to write a paper on Rudolph Bultmann, which is an exercise in and of itself. When he turned in his paper, the professor began to read it, and he said, "This is magnificent. This is good stuff." He was reading along, and then began to recognize some phrases that he had seen in another place. He went back to Wheaton College Graduate School and tracked down a paper written by a professor of theology there and discovered the student had taken that paper and put his own name on it. The paper came back to the student—"The author gets an A—you get an F." Pride based upon deceit. What is the antidote for that? Paul says it is praise. If pride is vain glory, praise is valid glory.

————————— Anatomy of Praise —————————

Notice verses 17 and 18. The shift is clear. "But, 'Let him who boasts boast in the Lord'" (v. 17). If you want to boast, boast in the giver of the gifts. "For it is not the one who commends himself who is approved, but the one whom the Lord commends" (v. 18). Not only praise of the Lord, but praise by the Lord. That is valid praise. Valid boasting.

Of the Lord

Boasting that is of the Lord means that we give Him

the glory. We recognize that all we possess is a gift. If you happen to be handsome and attractive, it's a gift. You didn't have very much to do with it, you just maintain it. If you have achieved great things, the Holy Spirit gave you gifts. If you have accomplished things, you were placed in a great land of opportunity. We have been given much, and the text would suggest that we give Him the glory, give Him the praise. This picks up on the idea from Jeremiah, "Let not the wise man boast of his wisdom or the strong man boast of his strength or the rich man boast of his riches, but let him who boasts boast about this: that he understands and knows me, that I am the Lord" (Jer. 9:23,24). He's a great God! Boast in the fact that you know the Lord, who is loving, just, and righteous. He's blessed us! When you are tempted to brag, "Boy, haven't I done well," shift it and say, "Isn't God good and gracious." Praise Him! Dr. Bob Smith of Bethel College, now retired, is a man who has always handled praise well. Whenever people would say, "You are the best teacher I had all the way through school," he just replied, "I want to praise my lovely Lord." He always refocused attention by putting it upon He who is the giver of good gifts. He is worthy. That's the first part of that text.

By the Lord

The second part of the text says, "It isn't the one who praises himself, but the one who is commended by the Lord." Project yourself into the final standing before the righteous judge. The people come. The first person arrives and says, "Lord, I've been busy on your earth, doing this and I've done that."

The Lord says, "I never knew you."

"But Lord, haven't I done all these things for you?"

He repeats, "I never knew you."

Another man stands before Him, whose name is Ed. I

met Ed in 1951 when I went to the Moody Bible Institute in Chicago. I lived in a dirty, dingy old dormitory called Norton Hall. There was a fire escape out my window, the room was small, the bed was hard, the paint was peeling, and I lived on the fourth floor. God was at work there, however. The first person I met when I walked in was Ed. He was an older man, gnarled hands, crippled when he walked, a bad eye, fingers missing. I assumed there weren't many jobs opened to Ed, but there he was. He made sure that we were all in by 10 P.M.—had to be. He had a fatherly concern toward us, and kept his eye on us. At night Ed would go down to Pacific Garden Mission and would work with the servicemen who came off the streets of Chicago. He'd lead these guys to Christ. I see the day when Ed stands before the Lord, in his humble way, and the Lord says, "Ed, well done. Enter into the joy of your Lord."

It is not the one who commends himself, but the one who is commended by the Lord. The Lord always takes His own recommendations seriously. If you are tempted, as I am, to have pride in your performance and to take the credit for yourself, we need to be reminded to refocus our attention and say, "Isn't the Lord good!" He is the giver of all gifts. The best antidote for self-commendation is praise of a great and gracious God. It will transform our attitudes, it will also make us a little less obnoxious. People who praise are people that you enjoy being with, they also bring glory to God. Perhaps you need to say, as I do, "Lord, forgive me for my inflated view of my own importance. Lord, I just want to praise you, you've been gracious and I love you! Increasingly I want to give you the glory." What a way to live! Then some day to hear, "Well done!" That's the bottom line!

Questions for Discussion

1. What are you most proud of? Have you given God thanks for blessing you in that area?

2. What words do you hope to hear on the day of judgment? How are you preparing yourself for that day?

3. Are you a person who praises? If not, what is keeping you from being one?

12

God Knows How to
Keep Us Humble
2 Corinthians 12:1-10

"I must go on boasting. Although there is
nothing to be gained, I will go on to visions and
revelations from the Lord. I know a man in
Christ who fourteen years ago was caught up to
the third heaven. Whether it was in the body or
out of the body I do not know—God knows.
And I know that this man—whether in the body
or apart from the body I do not know, but God
knows—was caught up to Paradise. He heard
inexpressible things, things that man is not per-
mitted to tell . . . .

"To keep me from becoming conceited
because of these surpassingly great revelations, there was given me a thorn in my flesh, a
messenger of Satan, to torment me. Three
times I pleaded with the Lord to take it away
from me. But he said to me, 'My grace is sufficient for you, for my power is made perfect in
weakness.'"

Some years ago Vance Packard penned a best-seller entitled *The Human Side of Animals.* It is an interesting study in which he portrays a number of human-like characteristics found in the daily life of animals. Take the homing ability of the pigeon, or what Isaiah recognized when he penned, "We all, like sheep, have gone astray" (Isa. 53:6). There is something about sheep; they follow each other, cluster together, and if one goes astray, they all follow after. Packard discusses the raccoon and the ant and the beaver, and a number of animals who have human-like characteristics. When you recognize that God is their creator and our creator, and we have a common source in God Himself, that's not surprising.

Recently some have noted there ought to be a sequel written which is *The Animal Side of Human Beings,* or *The Animal Side of Christians.* Two very unlikely animals have become very apparent in the church of Jesus Christ. The first is the worm. The second is the peacock. They represent two applications of a misunderstood theology.

The worm Christian. Many books have been written about the Christian worm—the one who really feels that he or she is nothing; there is a self-deprecating, almost a self-hating, attitude. Worm Christians interpret the Christian gospel as saying we're never to appreciate ourselves, but always put ourselves down. That is a misunderstanding of what is called Keswick Theology, which says that God is everything and humans are nothing. Failing to recognize that in Christ we have value and we do have worth, Christian worms are on the shelf, and not used of God because they don't think they have any worth or use. Then there is the other extreme.

The peacock Christians. The peacocks among us think they have a great deal to offer to God. They strut, and move among people, and in the Phillip's translation, "have an inflated view of their own importance." I must confess that some of the TV evangelists strike me as peacockish. There are tendencies among many of us to play peacock. Both the worm and the peacock are extremes. Both miss what God has for us. For you see, we are called to a balanced life. God asks us to recognize our gifts and celebrate them. Be grateful for who we are, yet walk humbly with our God.

─────────── **We Have Reason to Delight** ───────────

Paul says first of all that he has much in which to delight. In the first few verses of this chapter he talks about a sacred experience. Some have said that this was the most sacred event in the life of the apostle. He opens up the window, and lets us see a glimpse, and then closes it. You are left wanting to know more. He talks about revelations and visions (v. 1). A "revelation" is when God chooses to pull back the curtain, to reveal truth, to reveal a mystery, to reveal secrets and make them known. When the unknown becomes known the initiative is with God. God can reveal and God does reveal. Paul speaks about that.

"I know a man in Christ who fourteen years ago was caught up in the third heaven . . . in the body or out of the body I do not know—but God knows. And I know that this man—whether in the body or apart from the body I do not know, but God knows—was caught up to Paradise" (vv. 2-4). Verse 7 implies the man was Paul. He says, "I was the one; I was the one who experienced it," but there's detachment, as if he just doesn't want to draw any attention to himself. Fourteen years prior either puts Paul in Arabia, when God was preparing his heart in the desert, or possibly in Lystra. Remember what happened to Paul in Lystra? He was stoned. They thought he was dead. Some feel that he was, that he died and went to heaven and had this revelation of God, and then God raised him from the dead. J. Vernon McGee believes that, and a number of commentators believe that. This experience happened at Lystra, they believe, and the revelation was at his death. Whatever it was, we know it happened. We also know that it was a third heaven, which he identifies later on as Paradise. Where is that? Well, according to the Scriptures, there are three heavens. Calvin said that there were seven, I don't know where he got the other four. There are three in the Bible.

The aerial heavens or that which is immediately above us, where American Airlines, PSA, TWA do their business. That's the first heaven recorded in Scripture. It doesn't refer to PSA in Scripture, but it does refer to heaven.

The starry heavens. The second heaven is all of planetary life—the stars, moon, galaxies, the realm that astronomers explore with their telescopes and calculations.

The residence of God. The third heaven is the dwelling place of God Himself and the eternal abode of the believer. That's where our loved ones who have trusted Christ as their Saviour are. That's where the apostle Paul is; that's where my dad is; that's where my daughter is; I've got folks there. The third heaven.

Remember when the cosmonauts of Russia went up in Sputnik? They said, "We went to the moon and we didn't see God" and they thought that they had closed the case. But they were in the wrong heaven. That was the second heaven, He's in the third heaven. Paul said, "I was there, and I'm not sure whether my body and my spirit were connected, but I was there. It was an incredible experience and there are things I can't tell you about—but I was there."

Paul has this vision and yet he does not take an ego trip over it. He doesn't have a long series of messages on—

"My Trip to Heaven." I wish Lazarus would have said more after Christ raised him from the dead (see John 11:1-44). I wish Paul would have said more. By the Spirit of God they said nothing much at all. There's still the mystery, but we know they were there. One man has written that one of the reasons why we love dogs is that they wag their tail and not their tongue. Paul chose not to wag his tongue about a very special, divine revelation. He was there, and some believe that he was there because it was a confirmation that God had called him. In that special revelation God allowed Paul to see things.

For fourteen years Paul has known great inner delight in his heart that God had opened up and allowed him a special revelation. What are our delights? What does God allow us to celebrate? We all have our form of revelation, don't we? Do you remember when you first trusted Christ? For some of us that was a glorious day, I mean, talk about a U-turn. We were going this way, and all of a sudden we got turned around. Our lives went in a different direction, our attitudes changed, our friends changed, the church became our family, and all of a sudden the Bible made sense. Moody said, "When I trusted Jesus Christ, I went out into the park and all the birds were celebrating by singing." It is as if God opened up and revealed Himself to us and we entered His family. We'll never forget that day.

For some it was much more quiet, less dramatic, but real. Or it may have been a mountaintop experience. Have you ever been away at a retreat? The mountains arch into the sky, as the rippling brook goes by your side, and you open up the Psalms and glory comes down. It's real and you meet God. You have a special encounter with the living God—the Creator of all. The Word of God just comes alive. These are special moments of delight when God reveals Himself.

Maybe it's a surprise of joy, as C. S. Lewis described

it, where the Lord sneaks up on you and says, "Surprise—joy!" I ran across a tape put together by Campus Crusade—Bill Bright and others—with music and Scripture on it. I've been playing it in my car and my heart just sings. I've shared it with others and they say, "What a great morning I have had. I just worshiped the Lord all the way to work today!" Surprise—joy! Delights that God gives to His people. Times to celebrate. Well, Paul points out we also have reminders to stay humble.

———— We Have Reminders to Stay Humble ————

Human Trials

To avoid taking personal credit for all of our successes God allows trials. Whenever we are tempted to think God has blessed us so marvelously because we are so wonderful, God will try us. Paul says, "To keep me from becoming conceited because of these surpassingly great revelations, there was given me a thorn in my flesh, a messenger of Satan, to torment me." Look at that phrase, "a thorn in the flesh." Historically that has been taken either one of two ways, either spiritual or physical.

Spiritual. Another way to translate the Greek here is a thorn *for* my flesh. That is, something that comes to prick my spiritual dirigible, when it gets over-inflated. It comes along and keeps me walking humbly with my God. It may be persecution; it may be testing; or it may be temptations. Paul must have asked on occasion, "Who needs this job? I keep getting thrown in prison, they stone me. There must be better jobs available in the first century." Temptations—to leave his apostolic calling. There were persecutions, tests and trials that came spiritually and weighed heavily upon him that kept him from becoming high and lifted up and conceited. That's if this means a thorn *for* my flesh. Most of the reformers, Calvin, Luther, and others have translated it in this way.

Physical. Most modern commentators translate this "a thorn *in* my flesh, that it was physical. Some have felt it was malarial fever, a fever that burns the system, and sends pain burning through the body. It is like the pain of having your tooth drilled without any anesthetic. It just kind of grinds away, and becomes almost unbearable. Malaria was common in his day. Others have felt Paul's thorn was a speech impediment because of his reference to his difficulty preaching.

I think the best guess is that it was an eye problem. You may recall that at his conversion he was blinded. It is possible he never totally recovered from that blindness. That part of it stayed with him. You may recall the Galatians said, "We would have given you our weary eyes— would have plucked them out and given them to you" (see Gal. 4:15). As if he needed them. Or then he writes, "You see with what a large hand I write to you" (see Gal. 6:13) as if he had eye problems and needed to write in large letters, not like one who had good eyesight. There's also a tradition that comes down to us indicating Paul often had terrible headaches. Well, maybe they were related to his eye problem.

Whatever it was, it kept him from having an inflated view of his own importance. He said, "it was a servant, a messenger of Satan." Satan is the one who brings pain; who brings disease. God was not the author. Satan was.

Paul writes, "It came to torment me," and that's ongoing, continuous. It does not just happen once, but it's ongoing. He said, "I've talked to the Lord three different times about it." There were three seasons in his life where Paul said, "Lord, take it away from me, I can't stand it anymore. It is too much—too much!"

I wonder what God allows in our lives to prick us, and humble us. A number of things come immediately to mind.

Financial reverse. I have seen people doing well, who increasingly become cocky and sure of themselves. Then suddenly the foundation begins to crumble and there are great visible cracks and they begin to hurt. They lose their confidence and cockiness, and fall humbly before God. Or sometimes physical difficulties nag away and keep us from lifting ourselves up. These are all reminders.

Disappointment can be a thorn also. This happened to me recently. I had a stack of mail and on top was a letter from my publisher. It's royalty time and I thought, "Wow, great!" I thanked my secretary and said, "Praise the Lord." Then I put that letter on the bottom and went through everything else because I wanted to save that for last. Since I do not know until six months later how one of my books has done, I was so excited as I opened up the letter. I owed them $1.35. It seems they had more books returned than they sold. These are messengers of Satan to torment.

God's Triumph

In the midst of the torment comes these words, "But he said to me." Perfect tense. Reaching back into the past, moving into the present, moving into the future: But God keeps saying to me, "My grace. What people can't do for you I can do for you. I am sufficient. I will meet you. You're not going to face a trial that I can't handle. You're not going to face a test in which I will not be there with you." You can claim that. Look at a text like this and it is just as up-to-date as today's newspaper. Some of you are going through tests and trials. I know that. I've had my share of those. You hurt. And you are reminded again by our Lord who keeps saying to us, "My grace is sufficient for you." Always—today—claim it!

Questions for Discussion

1. What occasions has God given you to celebrate recently? Have you thanked Him?

2. Do you—like Paul—have a thorn in your flesh? Have you asked God to remove it? Are you depending upon God to supply the grace to help you endure?

13

Take Out Your Pen, There's Going to Be a Quiz
2 Corinthians 13:1-11

Take Out Your Pen,
There's Going to Be a Quiz   "This will be my third visit
to you. 'Every matter must be established by the testimony of two or three witnesses.' I already gave you a
warning when I was with you the second time. I now
repeat it while absent: On my return I will not spare those
who sinned earlier or any of the others, since you are
demanding proof that Christ is speaking through me. He is
not weak in dealing with you, but is powerful among you.
For to be sure, he was crucified in weakness, yet he lives
by God's power. Likewise, we are weak in him, yet by
God's power we will live with him to serve you.

"Examine yourselves to see whether you are in the
faith; test yourselves. Do you not realize that Christ Jesus
is in you—unless, of course, you fail the test? And I trust
that you will discover that we have not failed the test. Now
we   pray   to   God   that   you   will   not   do   any-

thing wrong. Not that people will see that we have stood the test but that you will do what is right even though we may seem to have failed. For we cannot do anything against the truth, but only for the truth."

The thing I enjoyed least about school was exam time. Some of the most traumatic moments in my life were introduced by two little sentences, "Students, take out your pens. There's going to be a quiz." All of a sudden the head begins to spin and the heart begins to palpitate in double time. There is a queasy feeling in the stomach and the palms puddle up. I always hated exam time. Never liked it. Yet the longer I live, the more I realize that it is like death and taxes. It is lifelong. Exams just keep coming. Paul, as he finishes the letter to the church at Corinth, says, "Dear brothers and sisters, I have two exams. The first, I'm going to give you is verses 1-4. The next exam ought to be administered as a self-exam, verses 5 and following." Let's look at the text.

Exams Are Inevitable

For the Christian, exams are times of scrutiny and testing. As long as you live you will come under the microscope, under the light, and be exposed. You can't escape. The minute you trust Christ, you will be examined. Your exams come from three sources; they come from the world, they come from fellow Christians, and they come from our Lord Himself. Think about it.

The World Examines Us

The minute you say, I have trusted Christ as my Saviour, the world says, "Aha, let's check that out!" You may think that is unfair. You may agree with the bumper sticker that says, "Christians are forgiven, not perfect." Have you ever been cut off by someone who has that sticker on his or her car? The whole thing is, we are forgiven, not perfect. But the world, nonetheless, says, "Let us check him out." They are watching. Think of it. Once you become a Christian and your neighbors know, the word gets around the community—there's a Jesus freak next door. The minute it is known that you have turned your life over to Jesus Christ, your employer feels there ought to be an improvement in performance. Your friends and your family say, "We'll give him six months." You don't have to invite examination, the world chooses to do it.

Fellow Christians Examine Us

Our brothers and sisters in the Lord examine us, *sometimes improperly*, often in the spirit of tracking and keeping score. "Aha, guess what they're doing now!" That is self-righteousness. It is viewing others and challenging their behavior, their activity, their habits. Keeping track of where they've been, or where they haven't been. Christians have a tendency to snip at each other. Now that is improper on at least two points. One, it presumes upon the prerogative of God. God is holy and righteous, and He can be trusted to make judgments. He does not need us for His sergeants—or a bunch of little judges. "Judge not, that you be not judged" (Matt. 7:1, *NKJV*). That is not a subtle text. That's clear, at least if you understand language. We presume upon God's position when we feel we have to judge because we somehow do not trust Him to handle it.

The second thing that makes it wrong is that it is always self-promoting. The minute you challenge another Christian, and ask others to pray about him or her, guess what you're doing? Usually these invitations are an approach to gossip: "We've got to pray for him, and let me

tell you all the garbage." That's gossip regardless of how
you spiritualize it. That is judgmental. It is taking God's job
from Him. But, it's always self-promoting. For you see,
any time you challenge another person's behavior, or call it
into question, or critique it, you are lowering that person
and raising yourself. It is a form of pride. Being judgmental
always involves pride. Criticism of fellow Christians is
always pride. If you can somehow challenge them, you
have said, "I am better." Or, "I'm not as bad." So our old
prideful spirit, the old nature, comes in. Self-examination
is all right, but examinations of others is often wrong.
Paul, in verses 1-4, gives us a proper examination of fellow Christians.

Our brothers and sisters in the Lord examine us,
sometimes properly. He says, "This will be my third visit to
you." Let's review the background. In Acts 18 we are told
that Paul visited Corinth and founded the church. After he
left he wrote them a letter (1 Corinthians) which unveils,
one after another, a whole series of problems in that
church. He talks about their divisiveness; their immorality; the way they misused worship; and the ways they had
not been good citizens. The church at Corinth was a very
carnal church. The world was in the church instead of the
church being in the world. After writing 1 Corinthians, he
went back to visit for just three months. It was a discour-
aging visit. Paul was not happy with the response, and he
left with a heavy heart. He then wrote what is called, "the
severe letter," discussed earlier in chapter 8 and 2 Corinthians 7. After he wrote it he had second thoughts but
then Titus came with the news the church at Corinth was
shaping up. Things were healthy at Corinth. They took the
letter seriously; and were responding to it. Now, Paul
says, I'm going to come a third time. When I come, I'm
going to give you an exam. I've warned you. I'm coming;
and when I come I'm going to make sure we have wit-

nesses to verify and document it to make certain it is clear you are going to be judged.

Now what makes his judgment right, and our examinations of other Christians wrong? Catch the spirit in verse 9. "We are glad whenever we are weak but you are strong; and our prayer is for your perfection." When we examine Christians we are glad when they are strong and we are weak. The motivation clarifies the validity of the examination. If your examination of a fellow Christian comes from a heart that cares enough to confront for their healing and their well-being because you love them and you want to lift them up, then it's right. We are called to bear one another's burdens, encourage one another, challenge one another. When your spirit is that of the apostle Paul, you simply want to lift them, and you don't care how you look. Then that examination of a brother or sister is right.

Examination of other Christians is also proper when you come alongside another in a spirit of humility, confessing your own weakness, to challenge someone who has gotten out of line. Read Galatians 6. It's also proper to be concerned for your neighbors, friends, and family; and to see their need for Christ and share Christ with them. That kind of examination is positive and motivated by love and care. That is right. Pauls says, "I care for you; I want you raised up; I want you lifted. And I don't care how I look." That attitude is always proper.

God Examines Us

"We must all appear before the judgment seat of Christ, that each one may receive what is due him for the things done while in the body, whether good or bad" (2 Cor. 5:10). The day is coming when you are going to stand before God, and give an account for your life. It is not a question of your salvation. If you have trusted Christ, don't be concerned about that. "Therefore, there is now no condemnation for those who are in Christ Jesus" (Rom. 8:1). But you are accountable for your faithfulness and for how you have spent your life. First Corinthians 3 talks about two kinds of results. Either your life is valuable like gold, silver, and precious stones, or it is dispensable like wood, hay, and stubble. Which will it be? This is the examination that is coming when we stand before God.

Remember the parable in Matthew 25? The master calls three servants before him. He gives one servant five talents, another two talents, and another one talent. He orders them to use their talents well while he is gone. When he returns after a long absence he asks, "Gentlemen what have you done?" The first servant says, "Master you gave me five talents and I have earned another five talents." The master says, "Well done." The second servant says, "Master, you gave me two talents, here's another two." The master says, "Well done." Then he turns to the third servant asking, "How have you done with your talent?" The servant replies, "Well, I still have it. I buried it so I wouldn't lose it." The master said, "Fool. You know that I'm an exacting taskmaster. I expected you to be faithful." And he takes the talent and gives it to the others.

Some day we will stand before God, and give an accounting for faithfulness. This is God's examination. It is also ongoing as we live under the powerful eye of God.

Self-Examinations Are Healthy

Notice verse 5 of 2 Corinthians 13 and following: "Examine yourselves to see whether you are in the faith." Test yourself. Rather than spending their time checking out the apostles, or his message, Paul urges them to look at themselves. Self-examination. Open up your hearts, your lives, and see how you are doing. If you focus your energies on self-examination, life gets squared away, and three positive things occur.

Faithfulness

Self-examination is a corrective to faithlessness. Verse 5 says, "Examine yourselves to see whether you are in the faith; test yourselves. Do you not realize that Christ Jesus is in you—unless, of course, you fail the test?" Paul is saying it is possible that when you look into your life, you may realize you don't know Christ, and have never really trusted Him. That is one exam you don't have to fail. Nobody needs to fail because the day of salvation is now. You can be born again, redeemed, saved, heaven bound, and become His child. You can pass that test. Self-examination could correct faithlessness. If you were to stand before God today, what right do you have to claim heaven as your eternal home? If you've trusted Christ you can stand in His righteousness; then you have a valid entrance into His presence. Test yourself. Are you a Christian today? Don't assume. Claim His provision and make certain of that now.

One of the great stories from the Old Testament comes from Daniel 5, and takes place in the city of Babylon. Babylon was a magnificent city with huge walls surrounding it, almost making it impervious to attack. The king of Babylon became arrogant and haughty. He felt nothing could touch him. He was the ultimate authority and source of power and wealth. One night Belshazzar, for that was the king's name, threw a splendid banquet, with over a thousand people present. They were having one great time, and the volume was going up. Have you noticed that when people drink they get deaf, and they talk louder? Imagine the decibel level in this hall with a thousand there. At the height of their revelry, Belshazzar ordered the goblets that had been taken from the temple of God in Jerusalem be brought out. So they brought the goblets, which were dedicated for sacred worship, and used them to drink wine in honor of the Persian gods. By that time, Jehovah God had had enough. Suddenly the fingers of a human hand appeared and wrote on the wall as the king watched in terror—*"mene, mene, tekel, parsin* (see Dan. 5:25). The king's astrologers and wise men had no idea of its meaning. No one could explain it. When the queen entered, she suggested he ask Daniel what it meant. Immediately the king ordered Daniel to be brought in. Daniel didn't mince words. "You have set yourself up against the Lord of heaven. He has passed judgment on you. The words say, 'God has brought your reign to an end. You have been weighed on the scales and found wanting'" (see Dan. 5:22-28). He said, "King, you flunked the test." That night Belshazzar died. And that night, Belshazzar faced God and was judged. He was weighed in the balance and found to be deficient.

Paul says self-examination could reveal if you have passed the test. If you have failed the test in the past, you don't need to fail it any more. You can trust Him now. Please do it.

Judgmentalism

The second corrective that comes from self-examination is found in 2 Corinthians 13:6, "And I trust that you will discover that we have not failed the test." I think Paul is subtly saying, "Enough of your judgment." They had been very critical of Paul. They had been very critical of the apostles. They had spent all their time checking them out. Self-examination redirects the focus of your gaze. You can't spend all your time judging others if you are looking into your own heart, making certain that you're right before God. Jesus said something about being so busy with the speck of sawdust in a neighbor's eye that you miss the plank in your own eye. It is a graphic way of saying, "Forget checking everybody else out: you've got big troubles at home."

Unrighteousness

The third thing Paul would remind us of is that self-examination will correct unrighteousness. "Now we pray to God that you will not do anything wrong. Not that people will see that we have stood the test but that you will do what is right (v. 7). Self-examination will reveal whether you are in obedience or disobedience. Self-examination will reveal whether you are walking in the truth or walking against the truth. The unexamined life is not worth living. When you look inside, it will be a challenge to discover what you need to do to please Him, to be obedient. We need to bring our lives under the scrutiny of the Holy Spirit, to look again into our own hearts and lives in the power of His Word, to discover unrighteousness, or righteousness, and bring it to the light.

One morning as I made my way towards church, there were people out jogging. When I came to one intersection a man ran in front of me. He was older, well-dressed, wearing matching shorts and jersey, a pair of Adidas shoes, but his socks were different colors. One was black and one was light brown. I tried to reconstruct the scene. He probably was retired and got up a little early to go jogging. In order to let his wife sleep he dressed in the dark. He went over to the dresser, pulled out the drawer and the two socks looked the same in the dark. So he put them on, and went out to jog where everybody noticed his mistake. He came into the light.

The New Testament talks about living your life in the light. Paul says, do a little self-examination—turn the light on your life and see where you are. Discover how you are doing. Paul's concern is that Christians do the pleasing thing. "I'm more concerned about you than about my own life," Paul is saying. Today, when we do our own self-examination we find His examination is not necessary. Do you recall 1 Corinthians 11 in that great passage dealing with the nature of the Lord's Supper? It says if we would examine ourselves we would not be judged. Self-test saves His test.

Picture if you will a scene. You are on your way home. As you arrive the phone is ringing. When you answer, it's an angel calling from heaven with a message for you: At three o'clock the Lord Jesus is going to be at your house. He wants to spend an hour with you. He wants to meet with you. If you got that phone call, what would you do? Any confession to make? Anything to hide? Anything to pour down the drain? Any reconciliation necessary? Do you know the Word of God says the eye of the Lord beholds all of His people? You don't have to wait until three o'clock; He's with you now. We live under His loving, caring, examining eye. Paul says, "Test yourself." Do you know Him? Test yourself, are you obedient? Do you pass? Or do you fail? And if you fail, you can make it up. You can pass. Trust Him.

Questions for Discussion

1. Are you under examination from the world or fellow Christians? How will you respond?

2. Has your examination of others been in the right spirit? How can you improve?

3. Have you spent time in healthy self-examination recently? Which areas of your life are strong? Which need improvement?

4. What has been the most helpful aspect of your study of 2 Corinthians? Thank God for His faithfulness.

Share with others the insights you've gained from studying 2 Corinthians! Teach *Confronted by Love* to the adults in your church!

With Gospel Light's *Confronted by Love* coursebook you can lead a challenging and life-changing study of Paul's second letter to the Corinthians.

_____

The *Confronted by Love* coursebook contains:
- Sound Bible commentary to prepare you to teach 2 Corinthians.
- Creative teaching plans that lead adult learners to personal discovery and application of the Scriptures.
- Helpful teaching tips to increase your teaching effectiveness.
- Reproducible in-class Discovery Materials that you can adapt to meet the needs of the adults you teach.

_____

All this and much more in one coursebook! Just $12.99. Order yours now by completing and returning the order blank below, or phone 1-800-235-3415.

YES! I want to share with others the insights I've gained from studying 2 Corinthians.

☐ Please send _____ copies of the coursebook for *Confronted by Love* (AB615).

☐ I'd like information on the entire Gospel Light Bible Commentary for Laymen series. Please send your latest brochure!

NAME _____.

ADDRESS _____

CITY _____ STATE _____ ZIP _____

PHONE ( )_____

PAYMENT:
☐ CHECK ENCLOSED ☐ VISA OR MASTERCARD

CARD NO. _____

EXPIRATION DATE _____

SIGNATURE _____